Crystal Companions

Crystal Companions

The Use of the Mineral Kingdom
Within Modern-Day Metaphysics

Marion Webb-De Sisto

To order additional copies of this book, contact:
Xlibris Corporation
1-888-795-4274
www.Xlibris.com
Orders@Xlibris.com
52462

Contents

This book is dedicated to my husband, Joe De Sisto. Like me, he holds a deep admiration for the mineral kingdom and is an avid collector of crystals and crystal skulls. His enthusiasm about my writing helps to keep me focused on each new project, and his love and support carries me through those times when life is less than kind. Thank you, Joe, you are my hero. I would also like to thank the people whose practices are featured here. Without their input, this book would have little substance.

Prologue

In the summer of 1984 I was first contacted by one of my angelic guides through automatic writing. At that time I was an extremely skeptical person who did not believe in anything that can be considered paranormal. Much of what I was being given was beyond what I could accept or consider was true. However, in one of the very early messages I was advised to learn about crystals. This was a subject that I knew absolutely nothing about, but somehow my attention was caught by this channeled recommendation. I did some research, made some enquiries and soon learned that there was a growing interest within a small section of the general public in the properties of the mineral kingdom.

My first crystal purchase was a Clear Quartz point that was about 2" in length and ½" in width. I had absolutely no idea what to do with it, but felt the need to carry it in a pocket as I went about my daily life. When I was at home and relaxing, I would frequently hold this crystal and sometimes just stare and stare at it. Having seen many exquisitely beautiful mineral specimens in later years, I know this little crystal point could not compare in size or grade quality to many of the crystals that abound across our planet. Yet to me it became very precious and it remains in my keeping to this day. It introduced me to a world of wonder and pure magic, the awesome power of minerals.

I definitely became addicted to crystals, a consequence for all who allow themselves to open up to these amazing spiritual friends. For the next eight years I collected many, many different minerals, some in their rough state, others having been shaped and polished. I was fascinated by the dazzling clarity of certain ones and often felt drawn to those that boasted vibrant colors and faceted form. Holding a crystal would bring a sense of peace and rightness, qualities I was greatly in need of at that time because I was going through a difficult divorce. I also read several books that were written about the healing properties of crystals and I became intent on learning the healing art of "laying-on stones."

However, I was unable to locate any accredited training until I returned to the UK, after living abroad for almost twenty-four years. In 1992 I began a three-year training course at the International College of Crystal Healing in order to become a Crystal Healing practitioner. During that time I was taught by a number of very gifted and insightful tutors. I was given the opportunity to explore and further develop my relationship with the mineral kingdom. This training also made me realize that the many impressions about crystals, which I had previously received, were not my own thoughts. They were a form of communication coming directly from the minerals.

One of the early projects set by my first year tutor was to keep many different tumblestones, one at a time, within close proximity to myself. For a period of not less than ten days I had to carry one within my auric field during the daytime and place it under my pillow at night. I then had to write reports on what each separate tumblestone had 'told' me. In this way and over the following months, I became acquainted with and exposed to many different crystals. I learned invaluable lessons given to me, I believe, by those tumbled minerals. This strategy of keeping a crystal within the auric field is one I would definitely recommend to anyone who is interested in studying the metaphysical attributes of the mineral kingdom.

As an example of what I was taught, Amethyst 'told' me that all minerals possess a linking network with their own family, e.g. Quartz with Quartz, Beryl with Beryl, Gypsum with Gypsum, etc. This connection not only exists at the physical level, but throughout all the levels of a mineral's being. Like us, crystals have different subtle levels of existence. Their Etheric Level is one that we frequently work with during healing with crystals and other therapeutic crystalline pursuits, even though we may not be aware of this fact.

Since becoming a qualified Crystal Healing practitioner I have been able to witness the endless gifts of wellness, harmony and tranquility that the mineral kingdom offers to us. I have experienced first-hand, both for others and myself, the very profound energy of crystals. My respect and love for the mineral kingdom has even deepened during the past ten years as I have added crystal skulls to my ever-increasing collection of beautiful gifts from the Earth Mother. These mineral carvings possess spiritual attributes that are truly astounding.

Crystals enhance, magnify and focus energies that pass or are directed through them. Knowing this, it is obvious that they will greatly improve any therapy, healing modality, or divination program that is being practiced. With this in mind, I have decided to document several examples of how I and other people are bringing crystalline power into our metaphysical pursuits. This book explains the ways we are further exploring the bountiful blessings of the mineral kingdom. It may also prompt the reader to find other methods of incorporating crystals into new spiritual ventures.

The various minerals, which are highlighted within the following chapters, should not be viewed as the only ones that are appropriate for the therapies, metaphysical activities, or divination techniques being discussed. They are the crystals which have proved helpful to the people in this book, but may not be the correct ones for others. Since the revival of interest during the late 1970s in the mineral kingdom, there has been a great deal written about the specific properties of crystals. However, from my own experience and that of other colleagues it would appear that minerals create diverse reactions in different people. What works for one person in a certain way may impact on another person in a totally dissimilar manner. Therefore, I suggest other minerals should be considered by those who decide to incorporate crystalline power into their particular therapy or divination practice.

At the end of the chapters, suggested exercises and recommendations are detailed which the reader may wish to perform. They are frequently set at a level which is suitable for those who have not received training in crystal and/or spiritual healing techniques, therapeutic regimes, or divination strategies. With the exception of the Reiki grounding and protecting recommendations, the need to be or have the assistance of a qualified practitioner is not required when conducting these suggested procedures. However, with regard to any of the therapies and healing activities featured in this book, it is important to remember that they are not being given as a substitute for conventional medicine. Seeking the advice of a medical doctor is always recommended when experiencing illness.

Light-filled Blessings,
{New Moon in Pisces}

Part One

Combining Crystals with Therapies
and Complementary Medicine

Chapter One

Crystal Regression Healing

The belief in reincarnation is nothing new despite its popularity within the New Age community. History has shown that some ancient cultures, e.g. Ancient Egypt and Ancient Greece, together with several eastern religions, e.g. Hinduism, Buddhism, Sikhism and Jainism, embraced this concept. It is the strongly held notion that we return, again and again, to take physical form. Even within early Christianity it was a definite tenet, but was eliminated from church doctrine by decree of the Second Council of Constantinople in 553 A.D. because it was considered heretical. All references to reincarnation, both direct and less evident, were ordered to be removed from the Bible. Several centuries later, two further church assemblies, the Council of Lyons in 1274 and the Council of Florence in 1493, once again, stated that reincarnation was heresy. These councils and the Spanish Inquisition successfully wiped out any remaining belief in it within Christianity for the next several centuries.

Although I spent many years being extremely disbelieving about anything that is metaphysical, I never totally rejected the idea of reincarnation. In the past this may have been due to my reluctance to accept life being a 'one shot deal.' That seemed so unfair to my way of thinking. Reincarnation also appeared to be a sound explanation for a distinct memory that I have carried with me from my earliest childhood. Within this remembrance I am a young boy, swimming in a river with several other children. This re-occurring and powerful 'flashback' puzzled me for years because I am neither male nor able to swim. More recently, however, I have come to understand that it is the memory of an event from another lifetime that has been carried over into my present existence.

I believe we all emanated from the Divine/Goddess/God/Great Spirit/Jehovah/Allah/etc. and since our first moment of being and, therefore, separation from oneness, we are endeavoring through reincarnation to learn and progress. We are following this soul task in order to return to our point of origin. Many of us have chosen to do this in very complex and creative ways, experiencing different life forms in both the physical and non-physical universes. We are projecting facets of our true selves, our souls, into many separate lifetimes. At the soul level, these incarnations exist simultaneously, but when we are in physical form we perceive them as being linear. In each and every lifetime we have learned both positively and negatively. These lessons have either helped or hindered our return journey to our parent, the Divine.

There is an infinite bond between each one of us and the Divine, to whom we constantly feedback the learned information. This link with our parent is never severed no matter how far we may stray from what is our intended soul path. It is a symbiotic relationship. We give back our experiences and, in return, we receive unconditional and everlasting love. According to the teachings I have been given by my angelic guides, the Divine is continuing to become. It has not yet reached its fullness. Therefore, within our concept of time this relationship we hold with it will last eternally.

Past Life Regression is a means by which our many incarnations can be accessed. It has become well-documented in books, articles and TV programs in which people's memories of other lives have been verified in certain circumstances. An early example was the case of the American housewife named Ruth Simmons. In 1952 Morey Bernstein, a parapsychologist, regressed Ruth and she recalled a previous lifetime as an Irish woman by the name of Bridey Murphy. The author Taylor Caldwell also underwent hypnotherapy. She learned about her past lives that were impacting on her ability to write in great depth about certain medical matters. Some people, such as Edgar Cayce, have been able to tell others about their previous incarnations. While in a trance state, the Sleeping Prophet, as he was known, correctly diagnosed people's illnesses and gave them advice on the appropriate remedies for their conditions. During these readings Edgar Cayce sometimes also referred to their other lifetimes.

Very early into my exploration of the metaphysical, I became interested in Past Life Regression and hoped to take training in this therapy. However, any courses, which caught my attention, seemed to be geared to satisfying the ego rather than gaining a spiritual experience. Such phrases as: "Find out who you were in another life!" often dominated the promotional literature for such training, and this discouraged me from enrolling. To me, regression to other lifetimes should be about gaining a sense of what I have learned and am continuing to discover at the soul level.

Eventually, my search for the appropriate course was rewarded. Several months before I began my studies to become a Crystal Healing practitioner, I took training with Denise Linn in Past Life Regression. This Native American woman gave many enlightening courses on various metaphysical studies during the 1990s in the US, the UK and Australia. I learned from Denise a method of accessing other lifetimes where negativity had been experienced and accepted through the emotions. Once these traumatic incidents were reviewed and the learned information was changed into a positive lesson, the soul benefited and its progression became more secure. I also discovered from my own and fellow students' experiences during the training that healing was not merely taking place at the soul level. It was also happening within the present incarnation's Physical, Emotional and Mental Levels.

While performing a number of regressions on people as part of the required case studies within the Past Life Regression course, I also began my training at the International College of Crystal Healing. After several months, it occurred to me that regression sessions could be intensified and enhanced by bringing crystals into the process. I reasoned that crystal energy should help focus and pinpoint happenings from other lifetimes that are impacting on the present incarnation. At that time I was fortunate to have a number of friends and work colleagues who were willing to offer themselves as guinea pigs for my fledgling therapy—regression aided by crystals. Therefore, I experimented and fine-tuned a healing modality that has proved to be beneficial and even life-changing for some people.

My first attempt of bringing crystal energy into a regression session was to introduce a Clear Quartz Elestial into the healing space prior to the arrival of a client. I had purchased this hand-size crystal in 1989 while visiting Hot Springs, Arkansas when I was returning to New England after living in California. I asked this Elestial to facilitate the whole regression process by dispelling any fears and uncertainties that the client might be holding. In place of these emotions I requested the crystal to promote confidence and a willingness to learn from other lifetimes. In my experience, Elestials assist us in leaving our physical bodies so that we can make contact with our eternal souls. When this process takes place, it becomes easier to 'tune into' our other incarnations. These crystals are very powerful members of the mineral kingdom and they carry the distinguishing characteristics of layered geometric patterns and etchings. Some have several terminations together with the main apex, while others have no terminations. They are considered by some people to have been gifted to us by the angelic realms.

After several sessions, I decided to remove the Elestial, once I had asked its energy to work with clients and immediately before they entered the healing space. I realized the crystal's properties had quickly imbued the area and that it was not necessary for a client to remain in close proximity to one of these impacting angelic gifts. In recent years and since becoming acquainted with crystal skulls, I have substituted this Elestial with a 4.5 lb Smoky Quartz skull named Metatron, but who is more frequently referred to as Tron. The carving style of this particular crystal friend is unlike any of the many skulls in my keeping. I believe the skull was fashioned in Brazil, but I did not see the crystal from which it was carved. However, its unusual pattern of coloration is reminiscent of other Elestials and I have always suspected that it was carved from one such crystal. Having learned from several years of being in the company of crystal skulls that their energy is more subtle and less 'in your face' than that of an Elestial, Tron remains in the healing space during a regression session.

Soon after my early experiments with the Elestial, I decided to bring earthing, or grounding, crystals into the sessions. The College taught me how important it is to utilize the energy of these special minerals within any therapy. Much of what takes place during healing is happening at other levels, and will eventually cascade down to the Physical Level. If earthing crystals are present, they ensure that this process is achieved more swiftly and with greater intensity. They also 'anchor' and protect both the client and therapist/healer while they have opened themselves up to the subtle levels of existence. It is particularly important for a therapist/healer to remain grounded during a session. This ensures that s/he is alert and stable while administering healing or some other type of therapy. A list of recognized earthing/grounding crystals is given within Appendix Six at the back of this book.

I began by placing a Smoky Quartz cluster at a client's feet or on the floor in line with the Root/Base Chakra, once s/he was lying down on the massage couch. Over the years I have learned to trust what my angelic healing team gives to me. Therefore, different clients will have different earthing crystals aligned with their lower chakras depending on the guidance I am given. This means I may use Smoky Quartz for one person, but Obsidian for another. Petrified Wood might be the correct mineral for a certain client, whereas Red Jasper works well for someone else. I have a 4 lb Red Jasper skull named Nedril who has successfully performed this earthing blessing for some individuals. In my experience, fossils are also particularly helpful in grounding people within regression sessions. They take us safely and gently to other times and other places, and they secure past life memories in our consciousness.

Even though the earthing crystal may differ from client to client, my own personal grounding mineral never changes. It is a Gold Sheen Obsidian wand that I bought in Boston's Quincy Market several months after being guided to learn about the mineral kingdom. In scientific terms Obsidian is not a crystal. It is volcanic glass and, therefore, is easily fashioned into spheres, wands, obelisks, etc. My wand is roughly 3.5" in length by 1.5" in width with beautiful streaks of gold on its 1" wide side panels. During a regression session I lay the wand between my feet. It has been a true friend for more than twenty years, keeping me grounded and protected during regression and healing sessions. Also, it is always with me when I am teaching courses and workshops to small groups or large audiences at holistic festivals.

Within Native American Spirituality there is a ceremony within which a person journeys to the Seven Sacred Realms in order to retrieve all of the scattered pieces of her/his soul. While visiting these other dimensions, the physical body is watched over and protected by the 'Grandparents.' These are usually other people or the honored ancestors. Having undergone this ceremony myself, I can attest to its profound and healing qualities. To me, the presence of earthing crystals within a regression session can be equated to the importance of the 'Grandparents' in certain Native American traditions.

In addition to the earthing crystals, I have added a protective and stabilizing field of energy to encompass the regression healing space. This was another strategy I learned at the College and I continue to use it to protect and maintain much of the esoteric work that I perform. By constructing a pyramid on the etheric level, any area designated for regression, healing and any other therapy can become a safe and sacred place. This astral structure is built around a client with the help of both an etheric crystal and those existing in our world. The latter are small clusters, tumblestones, or small spheres of whichever minerals I am guided to use. Within regression, an etheric pyramid enables a soul to revisit other aspects of itself, and helps me monitor and encourage this exploration. Once the session is completed and before the client gets up from the couch or chair, I disassemble the structure. I finish by asking that all of the dispelled energy be transmuted to the Light so that it will reach its highest form. This is a sound method of making sure subtle energy is not left hanging around and possibly causing problems. Instructions for building and disassembling an etheric pyramid appear in Appendix Nine.

Once I have helped clients to reach a deeply relaxed state, I may place tumblestones on some of their chakras if they are in a lying down position. At this point, however, I must stress that placing crystals on your own or other people's chakras is a powerful technique that should only be conducted by someone trained in some form of Crystal Therapy. Holding a crystal in your receptive hand *{the left, if you are right-handed; the right, if you are left-handed}* is a safer method of receiving this dynamic energy. There are minor chakras across your palms and fingertips and they will take in the crystalline properties in a gentler manner. If I do lay stones on a client's chakras, it is only for a minute or so. They do not remain in place for any length of time, as they might during a healing session with crystals.

I have found that either Azurite or Lapis Lazuli placed briefly on the Brow Chakra stimulates third-eye perception, which is essential for regression work. Malachite positioned on the Heart Chakra, again for only a minute or two, brings to the surface deeply hidden emotional scars from the actions of other lifetimes. This beautiful swirled stone allows these old traumas to be released and healed. White Opal placed above the Crown Chakra helps clients understand the karma that they have accrued in other lifetimes. I usually leave it undisturbed throughout the session because it is not actually positioned on the Crown Chakra. In healing circles, this chakra is considered to not usually need any help from physical stimulation because it is our connection with the Divine. Therefore, placing crystals on and giving healing to this chakra rarely happens and should only be done by a professional therapist. Yellow Jasper on the Solar Plexus and Sacral Chakras, together with Red Jasper on the Root/Base Chakra directs what is being revealed during regression into the physical. In turn, this aids the client to integrate other realities with the present one.

When I purchased the Elestial in Hot Springs I also bought a Clear Quartz point. This crystal has amazing clarity and a real 'buzz' of energy. Soon after it came into my keeping, several triangles suddenly appeared on one of its faceted sides. Having previously read that this phenomenon denoted the crystal as being a "Record Keeper," I have always treasured it. Record Keepers hold ancient wisdom from long, long ago. I usually hold this point while I am conducting a regression session because I believe it guides me to ask questions of clients that will best facilitate an informative and useful experience for them.

I also have a Brazilian Clear Quartz point that has phantoms within it, one etched in Amethyst and the other in Smoky Quartz. The scientific explanation of a phantom crystal is one that grew, then stopped, and then began growing again. Sometimes this process repeated over and over, creating ghost-like images of crystals inside the ultimate one. This unusual Clear Quartz point is kept close by during regression for the occasional occurrence of clients becoming upset by a recalled experience that was traumatic. I place it in their hands and it quickly restores a sense of calmness. It does not block what is being remembered, but appears to stimulate emotional strength and a resolve to 'ride out the storm' until the memory is completed.

In the early days of regressing clients, I attempted to capture their impressions and memories on cassette tapes so that they would have a record of what they had experienced. However, they often spoke quite softly while in a highly relaxed state, and some would say very little. What transpires in regression is for the benefit of the client and much of what is seen or felt by the one being regressed is not shared with the person conducting the session. With this in mind I decided to access a different method of recording the lives revisited. It has proved to be helpful and I continue to use it. Before the session begins, I ask the clients to choose a small Clear Quartz point. I explain that it is theirs to keep and that it will absorb the record of what happens when they are regressed. Next, while a client holds this crystal point, I instruct her/him to ask the crystal to take in all the aspects of what is being experienced and to maintain this imprinted information for as long as it is of value. I also suggest that s/he makes a further request of the crystal. The client asks to be the only person who can be privy to the stored information. In this way, if someone else should pick up the crystal, nothing of the regression will be revealed. The Clear Quartz point is then held by the client throughout the session. At any time in the future its 'memory' of the regression can be accessed by her/him while sitting quietly and asking for a replay of the events.

Any and all crystals, which take part in regressing people, are cleansed before and after each session. It is vital to understand the importance of carrying out this process when working with the mineral kingdom. Any energy that is being directed through a crystal, or to which it is being exposed, will leave a residue of that energy behind in the crystal. Therefore, if it is negative energy, it is of the utmost importance to remove that negativity as quickly as possible. Strategies for cleansing crystals, as well as some of the common causes of negativity in crystals, are documented in the Appendices. In addition, any crystals that work with me in any capacity are dedicated and tuned. Suggestions of how to perform these procedures can also be found at the back of this book.

One final request I always make of my team of spirit helpers is that clients only experience and receive what is right and appropriate for them at the present time. I ask for this prior to beginning a session and always thank my angelic aides at its completion. This strategy is a 'fail safe' that oversees the entire process and insures that nothing untoward takes place. In addition, showing gratitude to the angelic realms is an ongoing reminder that we are not alone and should appreciate the bounties, which are freely given to us.

Earlier in this chapter I stated that our lifetimes exist simultaneously at the soul level, even though in the earth plane we perceive them as having a chronological order. When choosing a name for regression with crystals, I decided that the words "Past Life" gave the wrong impression. From my own experiences of being regressed and from helping people to remember other lifetimes, I have discovered that it is just as possible and beneficial to access future and parallel lives. The latter are those existing within the same time frame, but usually within other parts of the world. I also see regression as a form of healing. It is pursued in order to release the traumas of other incarnations so that benefit is gained in the present life. Taking these things into account, I gave the name "Crystal Regression Healing" to the particular therapy I have explained in these paragraphs.

To end this chapter I would like to pinpoint some of the benefits of crystalline enhanced regression. Having originally regressed people and being regressed myself without the presence of crystals, I am able to compare the previous results with those of later sessions that included the help of members of the mineral kingdom. The crystals intensify and clarify what is being experienced, in addition to assisting me in overseeing and facilitating what is taking place. Some help to ground, or bring into the physical, the healing and soul truths that regression facilitates and reveals. Others reinforce the necessary close link between me and the client throughout the regression time. A client's visual perception of other lives appears to be improved, particularly when that person's 'inner' sight is not strong. I believe crystals ease tension at both the earthly and soul levels. This is an important 'plus' within regression because most people possess, to a greater or lesser degree, a reluctance to let go of the present. Quite often, a client is resistant to move into another time frame, another lifetime. This is understandable; there is a sense of security in what is familiar and constant. The crystalline kingdom lends courage to overcome what can be a conscious fear for some and a timidity of the soul for others.

When assisting clients to explore their other incarnations, I first take them through a guided visualization to a place where they are surrounded by what I call "the mists of time." Metaphorically speaking, this is a launch pad for the soul to briefly rest upon before taking off into another life. On a deeper level, I believe this imaginary place is a representation of our existence between physical lives. It has proved to be so comforting and nurturing that many clients do not want to leave it. In fact, some have adamantly refused to do so. Bringing crystals into the regression space seems to entice them to leave the mists and venture into a different incarnation.

On several occasions I have given Crystal Regression Healing workshops at holistic festivals and health shows. For these I usually position a large piece of Petrified Wood and a hand-size Calavera skull in the center of the room. I hold my own Gold Sheen Obsidian wand and conduct a regression exercise with the whole audience. Some of the people present will have brought their own crystals to the workshop and I suggest they hold onto them during the regression. When these workshops are over, a number of participants are always eager to chat with me and give feedback on what they have experienced. They are sometimes men and women who have been previously regressed without the help of the mineral kingdom. With regard to these people's shared information, I have learned they prefer the therapy I have offered to what was given before. They explain that the workshop's regression exercise was more visual, more real and far less traumatic than their previous experiences, even though the lives revisited were extremely vivid. This feedback has also made me realize that crystals act as a buffer against past/future/parallel life traumas impacting adversely on the conscious mind.

Perhaps the most important aspect of having crystals within regression work is their ability to help bring the non-physical into the physical. They make actual the soul lesson so that its meaning is fully comprehended at all levels of existence. This is the objective of Crystal Regression Healing and my mineral friends help this to become more achievable.

*   *   *

Exercise to Discover a Positive Quality or Skill from another Lifetime

Allow about 20-30 minutes for this activity. Either set some form of alarm or ask someone to alert you when the allotted time is passed.

- Choose an earthing crystal, which has been cleansed and dedicated *{see instructions in Appendices}*, also another small crystal that feels appropriate for this exercise. Make sure this second crystal has also been cleansed, dedicated and tuned to helping you with what you want to achieve.
- Find a quiet room or area where you will not be disturbed, and sit down in a chair or on the floor with your back against a wall. In this way, your spine will remain straight and, therefore, energy can flow up and down between your seven main chakras. Lying down is not recommended because you may fall asleep.
- Next, place the earthing crystal at your feet; you can actually rest your feet on it if it is large and this position is not uncomfortable.
- Hold the second crystal in your receptive hand *{left, if you are right-handed; right, if you are left-handed}*.
- At this point remember to insert the 'fail safe' request. Ask to only receive what is right and appropriate for you at this time. Also, ask for protection from the very highest realms.
- Close your eyes and take some good, deep breaths and allow yourself to relax. Playing music to help relaxation is not advisable for this exercise because music can stimulate all kinds of memories.
- Now ask to be given knowledge of a positive quality or skill that you have brought with you into your present incarnation from another lifetime. Do not ask to be taken to or shown that other life. It is not necessary to do that in order to learn the information. However, if it is appropriate for this to happen, it will take place. It should also be a positive experience if you have previously made your 'fail safe' request. Make mental note of whatever you 'see,' or 'hear' and know.

- Immediately after the exercise is completed, give thanks to the higher realms and document on paper what you were given. In this way, you are grounding the information into the physical and will have a permanent record of it. {Impressions, feelings and images experienced during regression can be as elusive as dreams.}
- Cleanse and thank the two crystals and have a cup of coffee or tea, together with a couple of cookies. This will ensure you are fully earthed and focused in your present incarnation.

After completing this exercise, give some thought to what has been revealed. Were you previously aware that you possess this quality, this skill? Is it being put to use or does it lie dormant? Are you using it for the good of yourself and others? Are there other positive ways in which you can utilize it? Do not let it go to waste.

Chapter Two

Elestial Reiki

Reiki is a type of 'hands-on' healing that was revealed to Mikao Usui during the latter part of the 19th century. This Japanese gentleman is often referred to as "Dr." Usui, even though he was not a qualified medical practitioner. However, he was an individual who treated many sick people and who cared greatly about helping others to achieve wellness. Therefore, it does not seem inappropriate to place the title Dr. before his name. There has been much misinformation passed on about Mikao Usui, his teaching career and how he received the knowledge of his powerful form of healing. Yet this has not diminished its ability to flourish and grow. The usual translation for the word Rei-Ki is "universal life energy."

Reiki was brought from Japan to the Western World by the actions of the following two individuals: Chujiro Hayashi and Hawayo Takata. Mr. Hayashi was attuned to the three levels of Reiki by Dr, Usui. In turn, he attuned Mrs. Takata to the first two levels in Japan, and later, in 1938, to the mastership level in her native Hawaii. Mrs. Takata introduced Reiki to America during the early 1940s and from there it spread to Canada and Europe. Again, there was incorrect information circulated with regard to the decline of Reiki in Japan and, therefore, the need to sustain it in the Western World.

Over the next several decades of the 20th century, what became known as Traditional Usui Reiki was shrouded in great secrecy. Students, who wished to gain the first and second levels of this therapy, were sworn to silence about the attunement procedure. The symbols and hand positions for giving Reiki healing to clients were also to be confined to memory and not documented anywhere by those learning this healing modality. The third/mastership level was only available to students who could afford to pay thousands of dollars for the attunement and training that would enable them, in turn, to attune others. Therefore, Reiki moved into the realms of elitism, which was very different from its initial premise.

In 1995, the women's spirituality writer, Diane Stein, took the bold step to break the tight hold the Traditional Usui Reiki community had on this form of healing. Her book *Essential Reiki* was published that year and it dispelled all the mystery and exclusivity that had built up over the years. Diane had been attuned traditionally and had also pursued other forms of Reiki that were beginning to evolve. She documented the hand positions, the symbols and attunement procedures for her own type of healing, which she termed, "Essential Reiki." Once her book was available to the general public, the high cost of Reiki training and attunements began to tumble and its secrecy was blasted wide open. She gave this powerful healing process back to everyone, as I feel certain Dr. Usui originally intended it to be used.

As a good friend, Diane was always interested in attuning me to Essential Reiki, but we were living in different states when she reached the mastership level. Several months later, I moved back to the UK and the opportunity for her to give me the attunements was gone. However, in 1997 a young Englishman named Paul visited Diane at her Florida home in order to receive the third level attunement to Essential Reiki. Previously, he had been attuned to the Usui Traditional Levels I and II in England. After reading *Essential Reiki*, he contacted Diane and made arrangements to travel to the US in order to visit her and gain the final level.

Once Diane had attuned Paul to that mastership level, she asked him to attune me on his return to the UK. He agreed and in the spring of 1997 both my husband and I began receiving the training and attunements to Reiki from him. What Paul gave to us was a mixture of Essential Reiki and Traditional Usui Reiki. For example, he taught us the Traditional Usui Reiki Hon-Sha-Ze-Sho-Nen symbol, but the Essential Reiki Dai-Ko-Myo. When I had completed the training, I attuned a number of people to the first level. They were taking a year-long spiritual development course with me at the time. By doing this I gained practice in passing attunements, and I also gifted to others something that had been freely given to me. I have always believed in maintaining balance in the universe.

After several months of attuning students to Level I and some to Level II, I began to think about bringing crystals into a Reiki healing session. On occasion, I had previously seen some Reiki practitioners at holistic festivals placing one or two crystals close to their customers. Some even waved crystal points around their clients' bodies before beginning a Reiki treatment. It was obvious they were intending to enhance the healing process by introducing crystalline energy into the therapy space. However, by observing them, it became apparent to me that most did not have a working knowledge of the mineral kingdom. Crystals were not cleansed and were positioned inappropriately. Also, if a practitioner was aiming the powerful point of a crystal at a client, the damage being done to that person's aura negated the benefit of the Reiki healing. It is very easy to tear the aura/subtle anatomy when a crystal point is moved indiscriminately within this energy field.

Therefore, together with teaching people and attuning them to Reiki, I incorporated the fundamental principles of good practice when working with the mineral kingdom. I gave some thought to a name for Reiki enhanced by crystalline energy, but could not decide upon one. Finally, I asked my angelic helpers for suggestions and they offered the words "Elestial Reiki." Since the winter of 1997 that has become the name for this form of 'hands-on' healing that I share with others.

Within Elestial Reiki earthing crystals are brought into the therapy space and used in the same manner for clients as in Crystal Regression Healing. They ensure that the Reiki healing energy is anchored into the physical body. I am particularly fond of having spheres and skulls carved from Red Jasper and Obsidian as these grounding tools. Next, an elevating crystal, one that is placed above the crown chakra, is positioned and is connected to the earthing crystal with intention. This further enables the flow of healing energy to reach all the way down to the physical. The elevating crystals used are not large and are placed in the same position as those given for regression. I usually utilize a 2.25" diameter Clear Quartz sphere that contains some White Calcite or one of my small Clear Quartz skulls as an elevating crystal. {See Appendix Seven for further examples of this type of crystal.} An etheric dome structure, rather than a pyramid, is placed over the client. The impact of a dome appears to be gentler than that of a pyramid. Reiki energy is quite dynamic and nothing will be gained by overloading a client's healing experience. The 'how to' of constructing an etheric dome can also be found in the Appendices.

From a large selection of crystals a client can choose one that s/he would like to hold during the Reiki session. Even without realizing it, people are usually drawn to the mineral that is the right one for them. This crystal friend seems to bring a sense of security and helps integrate the healing that is taking place. Those on offer are mostly small spheres or large tumblestones because these fit comfortably in the hand and have no sharp points that might hurt when, as sometimes happens, a person grips the crystal quite tightly. If a client does not feel adversely toward a carved mineral skull, a reaction sometimes encountered because of the negative connotation put on the skull image, s/he can choose from my collection of small crystal skulls.

Due to the fact that I am moving around a client and placing my hands on her/him, I cannot position my Gold Sheen Obsidian wand at my feet or hold it in my hand. Therefore, it is placed in one of my pockets and I mentally connect it with my Root/Base Chakra. As previously stated, it is very important for a therapist to remain grounded while administering to clients. During holistic festivals I have witnessed several practitioners becoming ungrounded when giving Reiki healing. This, in turn, causes the client to be ungrounded. On a number of occasions I have watched people stand up after receiving Reiki healing and they experience light-headiness and a loss of balance due to having become extremely ungrounded. Reiki energy is very powerful and can easily make people feel 'spacey.'

Soon after deciding to bring crystals into a Reiki session, it occurred to me that the attunement process might also be enhanced by crystalline energy. I began placing a large, natural chunk of Black Obsidian under the chair in which students sat to receive the attunements. This mineral was positioned on the floor in line with a student's Root/Base Chakra. Then I thought about tracing the symbols that are placed into a student's Crown Chakra and hands with a crystal rather than with my projective hand. Several years before and at the London Mind Body Spirit Festival, I had bought a natural wand of Obsidian. This unusual piece fits perfectly into my hand and tapers to a blunt point which is ideal for tracing the Reiki symbols. I began using it for this purpose and I continue to do so.

There is a growing interest in crystal skulls and more and more people are becoming avid collectors of these beautiful mineral carvings. This means some Reiki students are less inclined to feel unsettled by the skull image. Now, therefore, I sometimes place a 15 lb Tigeriron skull in line with a student's Root/Base Chakra rather than the Black Obsidian chunk. Adalan is the name of this skull and its combined properties of Tigereye and Hematite ensure the Reiki symbols are embedded into a practitioner's subtle anatomy.

About six years ago my husband purchased a 10 lb Brazilian Clear Quartz skull for me. I wrote in detail about this crystal carving in my book *Crystal Skulls*. Its name is Py-Ratti and it is a beautiful specimen with many rainbows and hollowed-out cheek and jaw bones. The first time I touched this skull it immediately stimulated the Reiki energy in my hands and I realized it would be an excellent companion for any Elestial Reiki work undertaken. If a client or student is comfortable with being in the proximity of a crystal skull, Py-Ratti is present in the area where a healing or attunement is taking place. This carved friend sits on a nearby table and oversees and monitors what is happening. To me, Py-Ratti is the physical link between me and my Reiki Guides, who adjust, enrich and stabilize the healing and attunements that I give to others.

A number of students, who had previously received attunement to the Traditional Usui Reiki, have come to me to learn Elestial Reiki. After I attuned them, their feedback about their experiences reaffirmed my belief in enhancing Reiki with the use of the mineral kingdom. They reported 'seeing' vivid colors and images and 'hearing' sounds and even messages during the attunement process. These occurrences appear to have impacted more profoundly on them than what had happened during the Traditional attunements. One student, who had received all three levels of Traditional Usui Reiki, never gave healings or attunements to others. She felt uncomfortable with what she perceived as the unbalancing energy of this particular therapy. This person was well-familiar with the dynamics of therapeutic pursuits because she was fully qualified in Crystal Healing, Color Therapy and Aromatherapy. After being attuned to the three levels of Elestial Reiki, she finally felt at ease with the vibrational energy of this form of healing.

There are several advantages to offering or receiving Reiki healing with the help of crystals and crystal skulls. These mineral friends provide a linking network that strengthens the connection between the eight levels of our existence—the Physical, the Etheric, the Emotional, the Lower Mental, the Higher Mental, the Intuitional, the Spiritual and the Divine. As a consequence, this crystalline enhancement ensures that appropriate healing reaches whichever level is manifesting dis-ease. Frequently, this stratum will be the Physical Level and earthing crystals help anchor the healing into the flesh and aid in its stabilization. They will also bring protection to both the client and the practitioner during the session. Whenever we are involved in metaphysical pursuits, we are opening ourselves up to the subtle levels of existence and can be exposed to negative influences.

In addition, because the mineral kingdom enhances and focuses whatever energies are passing through it, there is much less need for the Reiki practitioner to spend 5 or more minutes on each of the hand positions. 2-2½ minutes is ample time. As those who practice Reiki know, holding each of the positions for several minutes can become tiring, particularly for the arms and back. When a practitioner is feeling discomfort, pain, or tiredness, the healing energies do not flow as easily and completely as when s/he is relaxed.

In conclusion, just as Reiki can be enhanced by the mineral kingdom, crystals can benefit from receiving the Reiki healing energy and/or attunements. When a crystal has been misused or negativity has built up inside it, a Reiki practitioner can heal and re-establish that crystal's former purity. By holding or laying hands on the crystal and directing the Reiki energy into it, cleansing will take place. Similarly, if the First Level attunement is given to a mineral specimen, it appears to not only cleanse, but also step-up the intensity of the crystal's properties. Attuning shaped and polished minerals, e.g. spheres, obelisks, skulls, etc., to Reiki offers the advantage of realigning the crystalline energies that may have become unbalanced during the carving process. In my own experience and that of some of my students, exposing crystals to Elestial Reiki healing and attunements has proved to be even more beneficial. Perhaps the innate mineral signature that lies at the heart of this particular form of Reiki is promoting even greater empowerment. Crystalline energy joins with crystalline energy and boosts the needed effect.

*   *   *

Recommendations to Protect and Ground a Reiki Healing Session

If you are a practitioner of any of the forms of Reiki that exist today, try the following suggestions:

- Before the session begins, lay out a collection of tumblestones, small crystals, or crystal skulls on a nearby table.
- Choose a small, cleansed earthing tumblestone, crystal, or crystal skull from this collection and place it in one of your pockets. With the power of your mind and with intention, imagine you are linking this mineral specimen to your Root/Base Chakra, which is located close to the coccyx bone at the base of the spine. Form follows thought and if the thought is strengthened by intention, the desired effect will happen. By doing this you will be helping to keep yourself well-grounded and protected while the Reiki energy flows through you and into your client. If at any time during the session you feel ungrounded, either touch the tumblestone/crystal/crystal skull with your receptive hand or mentally make contact with it.

- Once your client is lying comfortably on the massage couch and before you begin giving her/him the Reiki treatment, choose another cleansed earthing tumblestone, crystal, or crystal skull from your collection.
- Place it just below your client's feet and, once again, with both the power of your mind and intention, imagine you are linking this mineral specimen to your client's Root/Base Chakra. This strategy will reinforce grounding and protection for your client. It will also help anchor the healing energy into the client's physical body.
- Do not forget to insert the 'fail safe' request for your client, i.e. that s/he only receives what is right and appropriate for her/him at this time.
- When the session is finished, but before the client gets up from the couch, remove the earthing tumblestone/crystal/crystal skull.
- Remember to cleanse and thank the earthing mineral specimens that have helped ground and protect you and your client during the Reiki session.

Chapter Three

Gem and Flower Elixirs

The use of elixirs to promote healing has been pursued for thousands of years. The Australian Aborigines, the Native Americans and the Ancient Egyptians all trusted flower essences to change a person's vibrational energy in order to cure sickness. The essence of a plant was extracted by placing flowers in water-filled containers, and then allowing time for sunlight to heat the water; or by distillation during which the water was heated by some other means. These methods of infusion resulted in a potent liquid that could be stored, with the addition of a small quantity of an alcoholic brew, until it was needed to treat ailments of the body, mind and spirit.

Rose Water is one example of a flower essence known to the ancients. This clear, aromatic and pleasant-tasting liquid was used by the Egyptians and Romans to freshen the air within their homes and buildings. The Persians explored the culinary aspects of this delicate elixir, enhancing certain dishes with its flavor. In India it was used to season various desserts. During The Middle Ages, Rose Water was considered beneficial for bathing and hand-washing. When taken internally, it was also thought to be a remedy for depression. In the 19th century, the American Shakers savored the taste of the distilled liquid that they produced from their home-grown roses.

During the 1930s, an English doctor named Edward Bach created his Bach Flower Remedies® from a variety of different plants, trees and the waters of a spring that flowed in the village of Sotwell, the final home of this visionary man. Dr. Bach was born just outside Birmingham, England in 1886. He left school at the age of 16 and worked for three years in his father's brass foundry in order to put himself through medical school. Eventually, he developed a busy practice close to Harley Street in London, and also freely treated the poor in Nottingham Place.

As time passed, Dr. Bach became increasingly dissatisfied with orthodox medicine. He observed that patients returned, again and again, suffering from some new health problem or a return of an old one, even though his medical skills should have cured them. This encouraged him to rethink what he had been taught about the causes of illness. He came to believe that we enter this life with a perfect blueprint of who we are and what we are here to do, but the negative effects of what we experience, think and feel gradually conceal our true personality. This, in turn, leads to ill health. Dr. Bach turned his attention to Homeopathy, but continued to believe that the key to good health lay in a more gentle approach.

In 1930 at the age of 43 he closed his practice and turned toward nature for the answer to his quest. He lived in Wales for a time and discovered a safe and gentle method of extracting the essence from plants and trees. Later he moved to Cromer in Norfolk, then to Mount Vernon in the little village of Sotwell in Oxfordshire. From 1930 to 1936 he developed his 38 Remedies which cover all aspects of human nature. In November 1936 he died peacefully in his sleep, having completed, I am sure, his reason for being here. He has handed to us a wonderful legacy of how to achieve bountiful health. If we are willing to look inward with honesty and face our shadow side, then with the help of his Remedies we can reclaim our true selves. We can become whole.

In 1995, I took the training to become a registered Bach Foundation practitioner. I have treated myself, family, friends and members of the general public with Dr. Bach's amazing Flower Remedies with very encouraging results. However, I have never incorporated crystals into any aspect of working with these plant elixirs. This is partly due to the fact that the Code of Conduct, to which I must adhere in order to remain registered, requires me to keep any undertaking with the Remedies free from additional trappings. Dr. Bach advocated the purity and simplicity of his healing modality and, therefore, Bach practitioners are not allowed to waiver from his philosophy when utilizing it. Yet even if this was not a required practice, it is very doubtful that I would bring other elements into my work with the Bach Flower Remedies. They are powerful and complete within themselves and have no need for possible enhancers. However, I have created some of my own flower and gem essences from certain flowers that grow in my garden and a selection of the many crystals that keep company with me in my home.

Other people have also discovered the benefit of adding the essence of crystals to those of the plant kingdom. There are a number of flower and gem essences available for purchase at holistic festivals, health shows and via the Internet. If you search for "Flower and Gem Essences" on Google, you will be shown an extensive list. Try any that appeal to you, but also explore the possibility of making your own. I would encourage anyone, who reads this book, to experiment with this fascinating approach to achieving good health. With this in mind, I am including an exercise at the end of this chapter which gives instructions on how to marry the healing energies of plants, crystals and the sun for your own well-being.

Lisa Trevethan is a woman I met online through a Yahoo group of crystal skull caretakers. For several years she has been making her own brand of gemstone and vibrational essences, oils and mists. I asked her to give a brief outline of how she creates some of these powerful products and below is what she sent to me.

Lisa's Process for Creating Her Gemstone Essences:

- "When I create gem/mineral essences, I take a bottle that has been filled with the preservative solution of 50% raspberry vodka and 50% spring water; that has a Chlorite included Quartz icosahedron in the solution, has been blessed to the user's highest good, has had light energy run through it and has spent time in a copper pyramid.

- I take the bottle and the stone into a sacred space that has been cleansed with incense and space clearing mist, and then enhanced with a sacred space mist. I center, ground, protect and call in guides. I then establish contact with the deva of the stone the essence is being created from. I ask the deva if it is willing to work with me, and then ask the deva to connect to the Overlighting Deva of the stone I am working with. The stone then becomes a filter, or gateway, for the energies of the source deva. That way I don't deplete the energies of the stone.

- Once I have permission and contact with the Overlighting Deva has been established, I place the stone in my left palm with the essence bottle in my right hand above the stone. The energy flows from the Overlighting Deva to the deva of the stone. I take into my left palm and out the right, sending the energy into the bottle. It is like a circuit. The water is then infused with the vibrational pattern of the stone. This method is for a single stone mother essence.

- I also co-create multiple stone essences that are not essence blends, but blended stone energies. When I create those, I take the stones that will co-create the essence and place them around the mother bottle. I have a Selenite wand I use to connect the stone energies in a circuit to each other and to the bottle. I ask each stone to send out a small beam of energy. I then take those beams, connect them to each other in a clockwise circle, like threads, and continue with the wand in a clockwise and upward motion. The resulting energy is then directed into the bottle with my hands because it is sort of swirling outside the bottle after the wand work."

Lisa has also worked with stone devas in order to "attenuate essence energy." Here is an example from her:

- "The Integrating & Accelerating Emerging Light Essence Blend is a blend of Herkimer Diamond Essence, Quartz Diamond Dragon Essence, White Diamond Dragon Essence, and Faery Luminosity Essence, and is attenuated by the Honduran Pinfire Opal Deva. This essence not only creates and infuses our entire structure with light, it also aids in the integration and further acceleration of the processing of light. At times, when one is drawing much light to themselves through different meditations, energy work, essences etc., the system can get overloaded and can be thrown into a healing crisis, or one can become very disoriented, spacey, or ungrounded. This essence will help to modulate and process the light frequencies to levels the individual can handle, and will accelerate this process as light levels and tolerances are balanced. The Honduran Pinfire Opal Deva attenuates the energies of the essence blend, but the stone signature is not part of the essence. The stone deva itself helps to refine the energy signatures of the blended essences to create a modulated energy signature. The essences that go into the blend help to draw light and infuse light into the body and cells. The Honduran Pinfire Opal Deva helps to tone down or modulate the energies so one doesn't get overloaded or go into healing crisis."

If you would like to learn more about these fascinating gemstone and vibrational essences, go to Lisa's online store. The URL for her website is given after the Appendices and Bibliography {see the section: Relevant Contact Details of the Featured People and Training Facilities in this Book}.

*   *   *

Exercise to Create a Flower and Gem Essence

It is necessary to conduct this exercise on a day that has lengthy time periods of full sunshine, and preferably when the moon is in its waxing phase. You will need a sterilized glass bowl with a diameter of no less than 8", a sufficient quantity of spring water to fill the bowl, a number of rose petals, a cleansed crystal, also a sterilized glass, jug and bottle. If the bottle is not large, you may need more than one. Before beginning you should decide which crystal and blooms you will be using from those that are available and accessible to you. To begin:

- Fill the bowl almost to the top with the spring water.
- Place the chosen crystal into the glass and then position it in the center of the bowl, making sure the rim of the glass is higher than the level of the water. This is a safer method than placing the crystal directly into the water. There may be residues of other toxic minerals on the surface of the crystal, or you may inadvertently choose a crystal that is, itself, physically harmful, e.g. arsenic, sulfur. Using the glass will prevent any toxicity bleeding into the water.
- Gather several rose blooms from the same bush. Do not choose buds, those that are past their prime, or any that appear blighted in any manner. Only pick rose heads that are healthy looking and in full bloom.
- Discard the extreme outer petals, and then place enough of the remaining petals to completely cover the surface of the water that surrounds the glass.
- Sit for a few minutes with eyes closed while holding the bowl. Ask that the enhancing energies of the crystal pass through the glass, and then enter the water in order to focus and increase the properties of the rose essence that will be transferred into the water. Also ask for the crystal's own healing energies to be added to the liquid.
- Take the bowl outdoors and position it in a place where it can be left undisturbed and will receive direct sunshine for a minimum of three hours. A longer period of time is also appropriate, particularly if the full sunshine is interrupted by the odd cloud or two.
- Bring the bowl indoors and remove the glass with the crystal inside. Also, scoop off petals and discard.
- Add a few drops of brandy to help preserve the liquid.

- Pour liquid into the jug, and then pour into the bottle(s).
- Secure the bottle(s) with cork stopper(s) or metal cap(s).
- During hot weather keep the bottle(s) in the refrigerator.
- Do not forget to cleanse the crystal and give thanks to the plant and mineral kingdoms.

You have now created the mother tincture which can be used directly from the bottle(s), or can be poured into small dropper bottles and/or those with a pipette. Store in a cool place and away from direct sunlight.

Directions for use: Place two drops of the flower and gem essence into a glass of cold water. Repeat several times each day. Over time, see if you can establish how this flower and gemstone essence is affecting you. Are you feeling physically better? Has it changed your emotional outlook or mindset about certain things?

Chapter Four

Crystal Therapy

The mineral kingdom is a vital part of our planet. Crystals and minerals formed when Earth was in the early stages of becoming the beautiful blue orb we can see from space today. It is believed that certain ancient cultures worked with the minerals and knew about their properties. They are associated with the lost continents of Mu and Atlantis, and some believe it was the misuse of Lazurite that caused the downfall of the latter country. Lazurite is one of the four components of the lovely stone Lapis Lazuli. It is also thought that some ancient pyramids were clad in copper and had crystal capstones to enhance their pyramidal energy. A theory about the strange happenings within what is known as the Bermuda Triangle suggests one such capstone lies deep beneath the waves. It is possible that its emissions may interfere with the instruments of planes and ships that travel in that area and causes them to lose their bearings. If by any chance the crystal capstone was created from Lodestone/Magnetite, then this theory is even more believable because those crystalline emanations would be coming from a mineral that is known to be magnetic. Another belief put forward about this underwater capstone considers it to be a portal to another dimension of reality. Some people, who have journeyed over the location of the capstone, are thought to have been thrust through this portal and, hence, their disappearances.

I, myself, have channeled messages about how crystals were used on Mu and Atlantis. The following are some examples of this information given to me by my angelic guides:

"... and the owner of a cabda on Atlantis. A cabda was a place of relaxation for Atlanteans. It was a building, usually of pyramidal shape, with many semi-large crystals fused at specific points throughout its construction. The placement of these crystals formed complicated grid works for specific crystal enhancement of the music and color of the soul. Inside the building were many small cubicles within which a person could sit in a meditative mode while his chakra centers were re-aligned and fortified. One of the many benefits of this procedure was the prolongation of the physical body . . ."[1]

" . . . Within another life on Mu, as a male, this facet helped build many makhus. These buildings were very similar to what Atlanteans later constructed and named cabdas, but their purpose was specifically for soul progression . . ."[2]

" . . . Crystals and gemstones were an integral part of the divine teachings of Mu . . . The ancient people of that long lost continent held Jasper as the most sacred of crystals . . ."[3]

" . . . and as a child priestess living on the larger of the two islands of which Atlantis was comprised after the second devastation of that continent. Crystals were brought to child priestesses to be cleansed and tuned before being used. It was believed that the pure, virginal essence of each young girl adjusted and heightened any lower vibrational energy within the crystals . . ."[4]

Aaron, the brother of Moses, was the first High Priest of the Israelites and he wore what was known as "The Breastplate of Aaron." This was a short tunic fashioned from a hessian-type material onto which several semi-precious stones were sewn. I doubt they were a part of the garment as pure decoration. Obviously, in those far-off days the power of the mineral kingdom was understood. As the High Priest, Aaron enjoyed a position of power and his special abilities would be enhanced by the presence of minerals within his auric field.

So it would appear that the ancients understood the properties of crystals, but over the millennia we lost this knowledge. Instead, we began to look at gemstones as indicators of power through wealth. Jewels in crowns, swords and church regalia, as well as those fashioned into jewelry, boasted of a person's supremacy over others because of her/his status in society. Only the rich and powerful could obtain such gems by conquest, barter, or thievery. Stories also abounded of certain gemstones being cursed or initiating ill fortune. As the centuries rolled by, the true power of crystals was forgotten and these beautiful gifts from the Earth Mother were ultimately viewed as only being displays of wealth, or as trinkets and fashion statements.

After the anti-establishment thinking of the 1960s, a growing number of people began to find an interest in metaphysical pursuits. By the late 1970s, the long-lost knowledge of the properties of crystals and gemstones was resurfacing. My angelic guides have told me that many souls, who were incarnated on Mu and Atlantis, are, once more, in physical form on our planet. Perhaps this is the reason for the reawakening of the knowledge of crystalline power.

As I explained in the Prologue, once I became interested in the mineral kingdom, I wanted to learn the healing art of "laying-on stones." The books, which I was reading, displayed layouts that were intricate and quite artistic. Having only a few tumblestones and small crystals at that time, I was unable to reproduce similar patterns of placed stones on myself. I also sensed that this form of healing needed to be studied and not just followed haphazardly. In later years, I realized that my hesitancy to place crystals on my chakras and various body parts was a wise decision. Then, I knew little about cleansing crystals and did not understand the awesome power of the mineral kingdom.

The International College of Crystal Healing gave me the opportunity to explore the world of crystals in much greater depth than what I had previously experienced. The type of healing this institution taught was similar to that expounded by the National Federation of Spiritual Healers, but was being combined with the use of the mineral kingdom. It was a perfect example of a healing modality being enhanced by crystalline power. Within the training I learned how to sense and 'see' chakras and how to gauge the energy flow from these etheric vortices. This particular process was conducted with the help of a crystal pendulum. I became acquainted with knowledge of the body's gridlines and auric field, and I was given many strategies to keep my own subtle anatomy well-grounded and protected. Another subject that I pursued as a student of the College was the need to balance the energy flow within the physical body. I was also taught how to create crystalline mandalas, grid works and etheric structures. In addition, my tutors encouraged me to develop the ability of identifying negativity within crystals.

Of course, I was also instructed in the art of placing crystals on the physical body in order to promote wellness, and I discovered that holding minerals within the various levels of a client's aura could equally bring an end to dis-ease. I and my fellow students were frequently required to conduct practical healing sessions on each other, and there were a set number of documented case studies, involving the general public, which had to be completed as part of the qualification criteria.

In 2003, the College closed its doors to any new students and presently only offers supplementary workshops and training to its alumni. In my opinion, this is a great loss to the metaphysical community. I believe the invaluable teachings of the College are greatly needed by those who are interested in learning how to practice Crystal Healing. However, the people who were fortunate enough to receive training from this establishment are dotted about the globe and a number of them are spreading its insightful philosophies and practices. Within my books about the mineral kingdom, I am also hoping to pass on the inspired teachings with which I was blessed.

Although it is more than a dozen years since I completed my training, I continue to keep alive and expand on what I learned by giving Crystal Healing to others and myself. It is not always possible to share with people all that I have experienced, but I do give workshops and training courses from time-to-time. Whenever I am teaching students about the mineral kingdom, I always make sure I emphasize the three golden rules that I was given by the International College of Crystal Healing:

- As a healer, or therapist, or whenever you are pursuing spiritual and metaphysical matters, always remain well-grounded and protected.
- Every crystal/mineral needs cleansing on a regular basis, none are immune from negativity.
- When using the power of the mineral kingdom, less is more, particularly if you have not received credited training in Crystal Healing.

The first rule cannot be over-emphasized. The College taught me that, as a therapist, I had a responsibility to remain grounded and protected while conducting a healing session. This was as much for the good of a client as for my own well-being. If the therapist is grounded and protected, this will help ensure that a client remains in a similar mode, as well as keeping the therapist alert to all that is happening. As I have already documented, when we give or receive healing, practice meditation, or follow any other metaphysical pursuit, our subtle anatomy may possibly be under threat. We are temporarily opening up levels of ourselves that are normally much less in evidence when we go about our daily lives. Maintaining our contact with the Earth Mother will shield our subtle bodies and keep our conscious mind vigilant.

In recent years I have become aware of the theory that some crystals do not need to be cleansed. In particular, I have heard and read how Citrine and Kyanite are minerals that do not require cleansing because they can maintain their own purity. I am not a person who thinks only my beliefs are right and everyone else is being misguided. I am always open to new thinking and fresh concepts. However, in my experience, and just as the College taught me, all crystals can pick up negative energy. I have most definitely seen and held Citrine and Kyanite specimens that were in need of cleansing. I can, however, believe that these minerals do not absorb negativity as quickly and easily as certain other ones do.

Perhaps the concept of them being immune took hold because certain people's Citrine or Kyanite crystals never appeared to become 'dirty.' One thought followed another and the crystal keepers concluded that these minerals were able to self-heal themselves and ward off negativity. This theory was then passed on to others and it spread. It may be that the specimens in question were never exposed to negative energy, or possibly their keepers were not fully able to detect when it was residing in the minerals. Having the knowledge that negativity is present in a crystal does not come easily and quickly, it takes long-time exposure to the mineral kingdom to gain this ability. Appendix Three lists many of the ways that crystals can take on negative energy. I am sure the reader will agree that these adverse effects are not exclusive to certain types of minerals. It is possible for any specimen of any mineral group to have been exposed to one or more of the documented situations.

As mentioned earlier, I was taught and have learned from experience that "less is more" when the mineral kingdom is involved in any undertaking. Placing many crystals on the body in intricate layouts is not necessary. Sometimes one tumblestone in the right position is all that is needed. Positioning crystals on the seven main chakras—the Root/Base, the Sacral, the Solar Plexus, the Heart, the Throat, the Brow/3rd Eye, the Crown—should only be undertaken by someone who has studied, in depth, the subtle anatomy of human beings, as well as being trained in Crystal Healing. Holding certain crystals within the seven subtle bodies of a person works equally well for healing, but, again, should not be attempted by the untrained. In addition to possessing chakras, we also have etheric grid lines upon which small crystal points can be placed in order to strengthen them or tone-down their flow. Once again, this procedure should only be conducted by a qualified Crystal Healing practitioner.

If crystals are brought into the healing arena, they boost, focus and strengthen the process. Yet when they are used indiscriminately, in overabundance and without a true understanding of their potential, they can tear auric fields, over-stimulate or shut down chakras and cause other long-term etheric damage. They can also prove detrimental to the aura and chakras when used without prior cleansing. Within the subtle anatomy, the Etheric Body lies very close to the Physical Body, almost like a second skin. When crystals are placed on someone's body, they are also resting within that person's Etheric Body. Therefore, any adverse happenings within that level, such as negative energy and damage resulting from the use of an inappropriate crystal, will eventually cascade down into the human body as dis-ease and less-than-perfect health. Similarly, the Emotional Body, together with the Lower and Upper Mental Bodies can also be affected by etheric negativity and this may lead to emotional and/or mental disruption and unhappiness.

In conclusion, I would like to give one final word of caution about spiritual healing. When offering this service to another person, with or without the aid of the mineral kingdom, it is very easy to fall into the trap of utilizing one's own energy in order to accomplish a positive outcome. It can happen quite effortlessly and without the healer's conscious awareness. This strategy may appear to work very well in the beginning, but will ultimately lead to a depletion of the healer's subtle energy. A trained healer understands that s/he is merely a vessel through which Divine energy can flow to the intended person. That profound power then stimulates the recipient's ability to self-heal and to achieve wellness.

*   *   *

Exercise to Experience Crystal Healing

Allow about 12-15 minutes for this exercise. Either set some form of alarm or ask someone to alert you when the allotted time is passed.

- From a group of tumblestones choose two of the same mineral and make sure they are cleansed and dedicated {see Appendices}.
- Find a place to sit where you will be relaxed and not interrupted, either in a chair or on the floor with your back straight and supported. Then place your feet flat on the floor to help maintain your connection with the Earth Mother.
- Hold one tumblestone in each hand and state that you wish to be given only the healing that is right and appropriate for you at this time.

- Now close your eyes and ask for Divine healing energy to travel right through you. It will enter via the tumblestone in your receptive hand, and then pass into your body by way of that hand. Next, the energy moves throughout your entire body and exits via your projective hand with the help of the tumblestone being held there. As I have previously written, there are minor chakras in the tips of your fingers and across the tops of your palms, therefore, the energy flow will enter and exit via these small vortices. The two tumblestones are directing the energy flow and you should not consider them to be transmuting any negativity that is being flushed out of you.

- Remain in this relaxed state for at least 10 minutes and note any feelings, thoughts, visual effects that you might receive. Be aware that the Divine energy is entering both your physical form and all of your subtle bodies, and is flushing out any negativity and/or adverse condition that may exist within them.

- Even if you are free from any such problems at this time, you will benefit from the exercise. It will strengthen you at all levels. You may be tempted to over-extend this healing session because you are feeling so relaxed and peaceful, but remember "less is more."

- Thank the Divine and the tumblestones and make sure they are cleansed before you return them to their usual 'home.' This action will ensure that no negative energy may have inadvertently become trapped in the tumblestones.

The exercise can be repeated, again, providing several days are allowed to elapse between sessions.

1. Marion Webb-De Sisto, *Soul Wisdom, Volume Two*, pp. 182-183.
2. *Ibid.*, p. 174.
3. *Ibid.*, p. 175.
4. *Ibid.*, pp. 180-181.

Part Two

Combining Crystals with
Spiritual and Metaphysical Pursuits

Chapter Five

Home Blessings and Space Clearing

My first experience of conducting a home blessing was in the late summer of 1994. While I was on vacation in Scotland with my husband, my only aunt died at the age of 84. She had never married and had lived all of her life in the home her parents, my grandparents, had bought toward the end of the 19th century. This house was in Coventry, a city in the West Midlands of England. I was born in Coventry and grew up in a house located only a street away from my grandparents' home. When I moved away from the UK, my aunt was recently retired and was beginning to experience mobility problems. Over the following years, she became an invalid and received assistance from the Social Services Home Help Program, as well as from my sister, who lived in Coventry, and then Warwick until her death in 2005.

When I returned from Scotland, I stayed with my sister in Warwick for a week. Each day we traveled through to my aunt's house in order to clean the property and remove all of the furniture and belongings. We were her only heirs and we had decided that the home should be sold. Although about a hundred years old, the house was in sound condition, but was in need of being updated and redecorated. There was also a feeling of sadness about this Victorian terraced building.

My great love of the mineral kingdom has always prompted me to take a few crystal friends with me when I travel. In more recent years, this means my mineral traveling companions have included two or three small crystal skulls. However, in 1994 I was not yet acquainted with these amazing carvings; therefore, I had taken several crystal wands with me when I visited my sister in Warwick. On the last morning of our work in my aunt's home, I woke up with a strong belief that I should walk through every area of the house, holding a crystal. In this way I could ensure there were no left-over energies anywhere in the home. On a couple of occasions during our week of cleaning, my sister and I had felt or seen the presence of two of the home's former occupants.

For example, one day when my sister was standing at the top of the stairs and was talking to me, as I was cleaning at the bottom, she suddenly looked very startled. She then told me that as she was looking at me, I disappeared and our grandmother was standing in my place. It was just for a moment, and then it was me that she was looking at once more. Since her marriage, this was the only home where our grandmother had lived, but she died some forty years before we were cleaning it. On another occasion, when I was dusting in the room where my aunt had died, I experienced a strong sense of her being in the room and watching me. This particular room seemed filled with negative energy, probably because it was where my aunt had spent several bed-ridden years. There was a fusty, stale odor in this room, which opening windows and the French door did not remove.

Before we had traveled to the house for that one last time, I had chosen my Gold Sheen Obsidian wand and my Clear Quartz point from Hot Springs, Arkansas. Being an earthing crystal and an elevating crystal, I felt these two would work in tandem, focusing the energies back and forth between them and keeping them balanced. I explained to my sister what I planned to do and she was agreeable. Although she was never a collector of crystals herself, she always respected my interest in them.

When we had completed our work in the house on that last day, I walked slowly through every room, upstairs and downstairs, through the hallway and along the landing. I held my crystal wands, one in each hand, and asked them to remove any negative and/or left-over energy from the home and to replace it with positive energy. To me this felt like the right thing to ask in order to make sure any future occupants of the house would not be troubled by any past happenings that had taken place there. This home had only ever been occupied by my grandparents, my father and my aunt, and with the exception of my father, each member of the family had died in the house and not in a hospital. With a hundred years of sheltering only one family, I believed the home was holding onto the energies from that group of relatives. Therefore, I asked it to let the past go and to embrace the future. I also requested that it be sold quickly.

When I was finished, the house seemed brighter and less sad. I looked for my sister to tell her I had completed the crystalline space clearing. While moving from room to room in search of her, I returned to the one in which my aunt had been bed-ridden and had eventually died. To my surprise, a beautiful floral scent was noticeable, replacing the fusty, stale smell. It was not a heavy odor, but was light and really uplifting. I presumed my sister had sprayed or put an air freshener in there. I found her in the backyard and I asked her what she had used in that room. She assured me she had not been in there and had not brought an air freshener with her. We went back to the room and she agreed that there was a floral scent and that it was much better than the previous odor. Both she and I commented on this unusual occurrence and we decided that the crystal wands had somehow brought about this improvement.

Soon afterwards, as we opened the front door to leave, we found a man standing there who was just about to knock on the door. He said a relative of his, who lived nearby, told him the person living in the home had died. His question to us was whether the house would be placed on the market because he would be interested in buying it. Apparently, my work with the crystal wands was quickly bringing results.

Once the probate on everything was settled, my sister put the house on the market. Immediately, there was much interest in it and we received several offers. We were able to then accept the best offer and, after about a century, the property finally changed hands. I feel certain my ritual with the crystal wands helped this process to move smoothly and speedily.

Prior to this event, I had gained some knowledge of Space Clearing and often practiced it when staying in hotel rooms or anywhere that was not my usual residency. However, I had never thought of using crystals as part of this process. I only used incense and smudge sticks to remove any left-over energy from previous occupants. After seeing how the crystal wands impacted on my aunt's home, I began to incorporate minerals into any acts of clearing negativity that I was conducting in various places. In later years, I took training in Space Clearing and Feng Shui. I learned why energy, or *chi*, stagnates and how to make it flow once more.

In 1999, I and a Crystal Healing practitioner colleague gave home healings for a number of people in their houses and apartments. I looked upon these rituals as a way of healing any unwanted negativity and left-over energies that were impacting on the present occupants. They also helped dispel any spirit attachments that were remaining in these homes. We used

Space Clearing techniques and crystalline power to clear and cleanse each home. Before leaving, I also gave certain Feng Shui recommendations in order to maintain the flow of positive *ch'i*. Both I and my colleague moved around each dwelling, burning incense, striking Tibetan bowls and holding personal crystals. We used them in a manner similar to how I had worked with them in my aunt's house. One of my Brazilian Clear Quartz skulls became a vital component of these rituals. She is a golf ball-size skull named Rell. I explained in *Crystal Skulls* how we performed these home healings:

> "As soon as we arrived at a house or apartment, I set up a temporary altar on a table, and this was the focal point from which we worked throughout the home. I laid a special cloth on the table, then lit incense and a candle and, finally, set out our Space Clearing tools. We asked the person living in the home to pick an angel card so that the chosen angelic quality would work with us during the home blessing. Once Rell became a part of the process, she was placed on the altar and, I believe, she oversaw and facilitated our work. One benefit I definitely experienced from her presence was a heightened sense of whose energy presence was attached to the home. This was something I had previously been able to identify, but not with such ease and precision. Rell also gave a boost to my work of sending spirit attachments on their way to the higher realms."[1]

As we live out our lives, both positive and negative energies are given out by the emotions we feel, the words we speak and the actions we take. This *ch'i* can then become trapped in homes, offices, schools, or any of the work and recreational places we frequent. It is especially important to remove any energy that is negative because, when left untreated, it can impact adversely on others who enter these buildings. Even the emotions and acts of bygone times can remain and negatively influence the present. This is why I believe it is important to remove such energy.

I continue to practice Home Blessings and Space Clearing techniques in my own home and anywhere that I am staying overnight and longer. I also use a scaled-down version of Space Clearing before and after workshops/training courses and in any rooms and areas where I am teaching metaphysical subjects. These can be classrooms in community colleges, workshop rooms in holistic festivals, or other people's homes. With regard to the latter places, I always ask for permission to conduct a clearing and blessing ritual. I consider manipulating the subtle energy of a person's living space highly inappropriate unless I have previously gained permission.

In ending this chapter, I invite the reader to explore Space Clearing in her/his own home or therapy/healing room. It is not necessary to utilize all of the suggested tools below, but rather experiment with those that are available to you. Crystals are a part of the recommended tools and they will enhance the Space Clearing process.

*   *   *

Space Clearing Techniques

The following tools and techniques can be used together, or separately, while Space Clearing.

Movable Tools:

Tibetan Bowls
Tibetan Cymbals
Tibetan and Balinese Bells
Other Metal Bells
Tuning Fork
Drum
Rattles
Hand Clapping
Incense
Smudge Stick
Feather
Water containing Sea Salt
Essential Oils—Atomizer Spray containing Distilled Water and a combination of Juniper, Rosemary and Lemon

Stationary Tools:

Music
Candle
Incense
Essential Oils—Burners filled with Juniper, Rosemary and Lemon

Large Earthing Crystal—Tuned to Cleansing*
Small Earthing Crystals—Tuned to Cleansing*
Wind Chimes
Sea Salt
Blue Corn
Copper Pennies and Copper Spirals
Water Fountain
Ionizer
Ferns
Sacred Objects

*   Ask the crystals to continuously help with the removal of negative energy, but not to absorb it. Request that they direct the negativity toward the Divine so that it can transmute into its highest form.

Using Movable Tools:

- Begin in the East and work clockwise around the room, using these tools. Pay particular attention to corners. Then use as many of the following techniques as is possible.
- Strike the tuning fork on a small piece of wood and hold the fork upright on the wood while walking around the room.
- Clap hands in corners at a comfortable level and intend that the sound travels up to the ceiling and down to the floor.
- When using sound, start louder and lower, finish softer and higher. Ring the bells and strike the Tibetan bowls. Use a two-beat when using a drum. Form circles or spirals when using the Tibetan cymbals.
- Chop incense and/or smudge stick smoke with a feather in the corners. Ideally, this should be an eagle's feather, but eagles are protected, therefore, it is most unlikely that you will have one of these. Any large feather you have found outside will also work well.
- Place a pinch of sea salt in a small bowl of spring water and flick contents of bowl around the room with finger tips. If preferred, sacred water *{see exercise at the end of Chapter Six}* can be substituted for the spring water.
- Spray atomizer's contents around the room.

Using Stationary Tools:

- Play music while Space Clearing both therapy/healing rooms and rooms for everyday living. The music should have rhythm and strength, as well as being something you like.
- If using a therapy/healing room, light a candle at the beginning of each day and keep it lit throughout the therapy/healing sessions.
- If clearing a room for everyday living, light a candle before beginning Space Clearing and extinguish it when you are finished. Candles can also be lit at night.
- Burn incense and/or essential oils during therapy/healing sessions. Use only very pure incense and essential oils.
- Burn pure incense and/or essential oils once or twice each day in everyday rooms.
- Cleanse and place one large earthing crystal in a therapy room and remember to cleanse it at the end of each day.
- Place several cleansed, small earthing crystals around a room for everyday living and remember to cleanse them regularly.
- Ideally, wind chimes should make sound by the action of the breeze/wind, but when this is not possible, be sure to touch/move them from time-to-time in order to make sound.
- Place sea salt, blue corn and/or copper coins and spirals in corners for therapy and everyday rooms. Remember to vacuum up the salt regularly and replace with fresh salt. Discard the blue corn periodically and replace with fresh blue corn. Also, cleanse copper pennies and spirals once a week.
- Fountains should gently gurgle and not gush rapidly.
- Ionizers produce negative ions that, in turn, create a healthy environment. Healthy ferns are Nature's ionizers.
- Only have healthy ferns and plants growing in therapy and everyday rooms. Remove those which are unhealthy and/or dying because they will create *sha*, which is negative *ch'i*.
- Whatever is sacred and special to you becomes a sacred object.

N. B. All of the above movable and stationary metal tools should have been cleansed by visualization** prior to use. Candles should be anointed*** before they are lit for the first time.

** **1.** Imagine that you are holding the tools under a Divine waterfall, whose clear, pure water washes away all negativity and transmutes it into positive energy.

2. Imagine Divine golden light is radiating throughout the tools and its beams transform all negativity into positive energy.

*** Dedicate candles to the higher realms, the Divine, the Goddess, etc. while smoothing a small quantity of an essential oil all over their surfaces. E.g. use Sandalwood, Patchouli, Jasmine, or Ylang-Ylang.

Things to Remember:

- Before beginning a clearing and/or blessing ritual, open a window, call in the Four Elements and represent them, e.g. a candle for Fire; a feather for Air; a crystal for Earth; a bowl of water for Water.
- If space clearing more than one room on different floors, begin with the lowest floor and finish with the highest floor.
- While Space Clearing, ask that any negativity be transmuted to the Divine in order to reach its highest form.
- If cleansing a therapy/healing room, Space Clear thoroughly at the beginning of each day, then quickly between clients. Do so, again, thoroughly at the end of each day. Also remember physical cleansing—vacuuming and dusting—on a regular basis.
- If cleansing a room for everyday living, Space Clear at least once each week, also immediately after anything negative has taken place. Again, remember physical cleansing on a regular basis.
- On completion of Space Clearing, cleanse tools with visualization and store them in a special place.
- Also and whenever possible, shower and change clothing in order to cleanse yourself. If not possible, at least wash your hands and face thoroughly.

1. Marion Webb-De Sisto, *Crystal Skulls*, pp. 27-28.

Chapter Six

Shamanism

Shamanism is perhaps the oldest form of healing. It originated more than 25,000 years ago within the Paleolithic hunting cultures of Siberia and Central Asia. The word "shaman" is derived from the Siberian Tungus word "saman," which is considered to mean a technique of ecstasy. A shaman was the master of trance and rapture, holding a position of dominance within certain indigenous populations. He was asked to mediate between the tribal community and the spirit world in order to cure illness, remove evil spirit attachments and to ensure good hunting and bountiful crops. His role was to become a bridge between the natural and spiritual worlds and to have access into the various dimensions. Shamanic rituals included singing, chanting, dancing, drumming, the telling of stories and, of course, healing. A shaman specialized in souls, knowing that fragments of a soul could leave the physical body and become lost in other realms. It was his task to go journeying in search of those soul fragments and to retrieve them.

Shamanistic practices are believed to predate all organized religions. However, elements of shamanism are found in Buddhism, Paganism and Christianity. The Tibetans, Mongols and Manchu adopted Buddhism and combined their innate shamanic rituals with Buddhist practices. Within Greek paganism the influence of shamanism is evident in certain myths, such as the stories of Tantalus and Prometheus. Similarities can even be seen within Christianity, e.g. some see the taking of Holy Communion to be a distant echo of a shaman's use of entheogenic substances for achieving spiritual insights.

Across the globe different forms of shamanism have been evident in ancient Egypt, Tibet and China. The Northern, Central and Southern Native Americans have pursued its ethos, as have the Australian Aborigine, certain African tribes and the Celtic clans. Shamans throughout the various cultures were healers, spiritual advisors, dream interpreters and herbalists. They also understood the power of the mineral kingdom. A shaman's pouch usually contained a Clear Quartz point.

This particular healing modality has survived even into our modern-day world, and the upsurge of interest in esoteric matters during the past forty years has strengthened its continuation. There are a growing number of men and women within the Western World who are treading the path of the shaman.

Shamanism is not self-serving; it is practiced for the welfare of others. It is also a convincing example of the interconnectedness of all life, whether within the physical plane or other realms of existence. In the cosmos of the shaman there are three worlds: Upperworld, Middleworld and Lowerworld.

The Upperworld: This is the spiritual realm. It is the place where the blueprints of life are accessed. Angelic/spirit guides and higher beings can be called upon from this level to give teachings on healing, mutual responsibility and true identity.

The Middleworld: The world in which we live. It is constantly overlapped by the other two worlds, and this fact makes it possible for shamans to travel easily from one dimension to another.

The Lowerworld: It is the home of our ancestors, the nature sprites and power animals. The very depths of our psyche, together with our deepest thoughts and strongest emotions, can be accessed at this level. A shaman works with the elements and beings of this level in order to help bring about healing, soul retrieval and spiritual growth.

Mark Loman is a close friend about whom I first wrote in my book *Crystal Skulls*. He is a goldsmith, an Elestial Reiki Master and an avid collector of crystal skulls. During the past six years he has also taken extensive training in Shamanism. Mark studied with Howard and Elsa Malpas, who offer training in "Warrior in the Heart Shamanism" in Glastonbury and London. He continues to work with them in a teaching capacity.

Knowing how much Mark loves the mineral kingdom, I have asked him for an example of how he incorporates crystals into his shamanic work. The following is what he told me about Extraction Medicine, which is one aspect of Shamanism.

Example of Using Crystalline Energy within a Shamanic Practice:

"Extraction medicine is a method in shamanic healing where the shamanic practitioner journeys within the Middleworld to find the spirit/soul of the person with whom s/he is working. This is done in order to find out whether there are any spirit intrusions attached to the soul that need removing. These can be damaging to the person's energy field and etheric bodies and can, if unchecked, manifest as a physical illness or as unexplained pains in the body. Therefore, it is important to get rid of them. They can be psychic darts, maliciously put there by the unloving thoughts of others. However, quite often they are caused by our own negative thoughts against ourselves.

When I do this work I start by filling an Agate bowl with water that I have blessed. I then journey, while holding a crystal on which I have performed a healing. I travel into the part of Middleworld that I call the healing pool. It is a shallow pool where I find the spirit of the client sleeping just under the surface of the water. I am helped in this type of work by two power animal spirits, Magpie and Crow. Magpie scans the spirit body while Crow stands guard because Middleworld can be a tricky place and it is always good to have a powerful ally watch your back.

Then Magpie spots an intrusion and points it out to me and this is where the crystal comes into the process. It's used almost like a syringe, drawing off the negative energy/intrusion. When this has been done it leaves a space within the client's spirit. Therefore, I call upon the animal spirits to find a power animal that will fill the gap and also aid in the client's healing process.

When this is done, I journey back with the essence of the intrusion held safely within the crystal. I place this crystal into the Agate bowl with the intent that the blessed water will transmute the negative essence into a healing medicine for the client. While it is soaking, I tell the client the story of the journey, my experiences and what I saw. Then I blow the essence of the power animal into their Heart and Crown Chakras, and I shake a rattle to seal it in. Finally, I ask the client what s/he wishes to do with the healing medicine. I suggest that it can either be drunk or poured into the earth, expressing that whichever choice is made is fine.

This is one example of how I use crystals and minerals in extraction medicine."

Mark is a powerful shaman who has helped a large number of people receive healing and spiritual awareness. He is yet another example of someone who has combined his spiritual work with the power of crystals. In addition, his beautiful jewelry also displays his understanding of and close affinity with the mineral kingdom.

*   *   *

Exercise to Create Sacred Water

It is not necessary to be a shaman in order to glean the benefits of sacred/blessed water. There are many varied activities to which it can be put, e.g. watering plants, cleansing crystals that have a hardness of 7 and above {see the Mohs Scale in Appendix Two}, adding a few drops to a glass of drinking water and to a pet's water dish. Other examples include washing hands and face after Space Clearing, or using in any activity that you feel would profit from the higher energy of this special liquid. The following is one method of creating it and should be conducted on a day of the full moon, preferably when this happens in a Water Sign, i.e. Cancer, Scorpio, or Pisces. You will need a ceramic bowl, a sufficient quantity of spring water to fill the bowl, a cleansed Clear Quartz crystal, also a glass and a jug with a lid. The size of the bowl will depend on the quantity of water you want to bless. If it is to be ingested by a person and/or animal, then the bowl, glass and jug should be sterilized. You can set the scene by clearing the area/room, where you will be working, with any Space Clearing method given in Chapter Five. Begin by:

- Designate a small table within the area/room as an altar.
- Place a lit candle, burning incense and the bowl on the altar.
- Fill the bowl with spring water and ask that only the highest, purest and most sacred energies enter the liquid and remain within it. If you prefer, you can ask that sacred energy comes directly from the Divine/Goddess/God/Great Spirit/Jehovah/Allah/etc. In addition, you can place a religious object, a Goddess symbol, or Pagan talisman, etc. close by the bowl in order to strengthen the intention of this exercise.

- Place the crystal inside the glass, and then position both inside the water, making sure the rim of the glass is above the level of the water.
- Ask that the enhancing energies of the crystal pass through the glass, then enter the water and focus and maintain the sacred energy that is permeating the water.
- Ask the archangels or whomever you consider to be higher beings to keep watch and guard the process that is taking place within the bowl.
- You do not need to stay close to the bowl, but can do other things, other tasks, etc. After 15-20 minutes, the water will have fully absorbed the sacred and crystalline energies. This time frame can be extended if you prefer to do so, but if the opportunity to leave the bowl untouched for a longer period is not possible, that is not a problem.
- Pour the water into the jug and, if it is not for immediate consumption, then add a few drops of brandy for preserving. If it is to be used in some other capacity, then this form of preservation may not be necessary. Secure the lid on the jug and store in a cool place and away from direct sunlight. During hot weather keep in the refrigerator.
- Remember to cleanse the crystal and give thanks to the higher realms.

Water carries the memory of whatever energies come into contact with it. This is why sacred water, flower and/or gem essences, tinctures and herbal fluids are so powerful. When you add a few drops of these liquids to a glass of water, the memory is then even more intensified.

Chapter Seven

Yoga

Yoga is an ancient system of physical, mental, social and spiritual development. Its origin has become somewhat shrouded due to the teachings being secretive and, within its early existence, orally transmitted. However, it is considered to date back more than 5,000 years and to have been birthed within the Indus Valley civilization. There is mention of it in the Vedas, which are a collection of written rituals practiced by the Verdic priests. Gradually, Yoga was further developed by the priests who also set down their beliefs in the Upanishads. These scriptures teach the sacrifice of the ego through self-knowledge, action and wisdom.

During the 2nd century B.C.E., Patanjali's Yoga-Sûtras organized Yoga into an "eight-limbed path." The text explains Raja Yoga, which is often termed "classical Yoga." This systematic writing details the necessary stages that lead to enlightenment. Patanjali is considered to be the father of Yoga, and his Yoga-Sûtras have become a strong influence on modern-day Yoga.

Several hundred years later, a new system of practices was designed in order to rejuvenate the body and to prolong life. The ancient teachings of the Vedas were rejected in preference of pursuing enlightenment through the physical body. This was the beginning of Tantra Yoga in which radical procedures of cleansing the body and mind would help unbind the student from physical existence. In turn, these physical-to-spiritual connections gave rise to Hatha Yoga.

In both the late 19th and early 20th centuries, Yoga masters began to spread an awareness of Hatha Yoga within the Western World. In 1947, Indra Devi opened her Yoga studio in Hollywood. This soon led to a popular interest in the study of Yoga, and teachers from both India and the West opened their schools to eager students. Today, Hatha Yoga has millions of followers who pursue the different styles and aspects of this practice.

Helena Albrecht-Esperandieu is an online friend who comes from South Africa, but is presently living in France. She contacted me via email a few years ago after reading one of my books. Helena is an artist who mainly paints in acrylics and egg-tempera, but she has an equal passion for etching. Helena also enjoys photographing the wonders of Nature. I have received a number of fascinating photographs from her that she has taken of trees, rocks, clouds and seascapes. In addition, she shares my love of the mineral kingdom and has sent along beautiful pictures of some of her crystal collection.

Knowing that Helena was a follower of Yoga, I asked her whether she had ever performed the exercises while using the help of crystals. She told me that she had not, but that she was very willing to bring them into a session in order to be able to give me some feedback on their impact. Her documentation on several sessions is listed below. Her reference to the vibration within a room is, I believe, an indication of the level of positive or negative *ch'i* in that space. With the help of a copper pendulum, this is how Helena, in her own words, measures the energy of a room:

- "I make sure that I am in the correct state of mind/energy to channel. I take off my watch and all of my jewelry.
- I light a candle for the angel of the day, e.g. today it is Archangel Michael, and also light the incense that goes with his energy: Benjoin/Sandalwood/Lavender.
- I put myself in a safe place with a prayer. Mine is making the Kabbalah cross before I start my work.
- I state my intentions and ask if is ok with them to continue. {I don't know 'who' it is who helps me, except that I ask for: "One of the Highest Light." I know that it is angels who work with the mineral kingdom, but I do not know the name. However, I recognize the presence.}
- I work with a pendulum, which I hold in my left hand for receiving energy. I ask if the energy is negative or positive.
- I have a piece of paper on which I work. In noting all the answers, I ask other questions, e.g. if the answer is that the energy is in the plus-range, then I will ask, "Is it more than 10?" If given "Yes," I

ask, "Is it more than 15?" When I find an approximate number, e.g. between 15 and 20, I will ask, "16?" or "17?" And the pendulum will tell me when it is "Yes."

Helena has emailed her experiences of bringing crystals into Yoga sessions and they are documented below for the reader's interest.

Session 1:

"I measured the vibration of a room without any crystal presence. It measured at 12, which is a healthy, good vibration. I then placed my big Cathedral Citrine in the middle of the room and the vibration rose to 22. This Cathedral Citrine is a very, very light color with Albite inclusions. Then I took a small Generator Citrine, which has a giant rainbow 'satellite' inside, and put that in the same place. The vibration, again, went up to 32.

I asked the Crystal Angels and they like the idea of having a Generator Crystal in a Yoga Room. The kind of crystal will depend on the persons concerned, but they {the Crystal Angels} prefer the presence of Citrine for me. I asked about Clear Quartz, Rose Quartz and Amethyst, but the choice was for Citrine. They also said that it would be good to wear bracelets on the ankles and the wrists. However, it was a clear "No" as to the use of crystals on the chakras during Yoga. So, from here I will now use Tourmaline on my ankles when I do Yoga. Somehow I just feel that this will help me 'settle' into serenity more quickly. It will anchor me deeply. I feel a great resonance to this mineral."

Session 2:

"I was trying to find crystal bracelets in Black Tourmaline and Citrine, but could not find what I wanted, not even on the Internet. So I decided to make do with what I have, and I am very glad that I did.

I used my Citrine Generator, 2 natural Black Tourmalines for grounding and 2 natural, rough Pink and White Petalite specimens from South Africa for inspiration. In addition, I brought a roll of hypoallergenic, non-woven stretch plaster-tape into the session. It is very soft and flexible. Firstly, I put my Citrine Generator on a little table in the East of the room where I was. The vibration went up from 12 to 27 in this room. I burnt some incense and I taped the Tourmalines to the arches of my feet, and the Petalites on my palms {as I was instructed by the Crystal Angels}. Then I sat down in the lotus position and just breathed.

The first thing that I noticed, which was different, was the rapidity of connection to One. {It is like the difference between dial-up Internet and having the cable.} Through my third eye I saw colors and forms, and then it settled into being a ball of yellow surrounded by a wonderfully, soft glowing green. It felt so good just sitting there that I almost forgot to move. I find it is a terrific way of moving into a meditative type of Yoga. {Perhaps it was because of the type of crystals I was using?} But, it did not stop me from concentrating on the movements at all.

Because of my operation wound I still cannot do all that I normally do, but stayed with the simpler sitting poses, spinal twists and a few standing up poses. In doing, e.g. The Eagle pose, I found no problem to focus in balancing, even with my eyes closed. After the little session I felt very clear headed and relaxed and grounded. Normally, I feel very relaxed, so I can definitely add the other two aspects to this experience.

I would love to find bracelets for both the ankles and wrists. That is the ideal. I will have to look in South Africa to see what I can find because I am going to continue the use of the crystal companions in my Yoga sessions. It will be very interesting to see how other crystals interact with each other during such a session."

Session 3:

"It has been a bit of a break with the crystals. Most of them have been out for cleaning and recharging before and during the full moon. They felt nicely refreshed after the time.

So last week I had another session and I decided to change the crystals on the wrist, but to stay with the Tourmalines on the feet. I chose to work with two tumbled Clear Quartz crystals, they are almost transparent. Like the previous time, I did my preparation with burning some incense and settling down with the crystals strapped down with the special tape. The Citrine Generator was in place and {my, oh, my} that crystal is a marvel! The Tourmalines felt really supportive, but to my surprise I had very little reaction from the Quartz on my wrists. Unlike the Petalite, they just stayed kind of quiet. I was aware of a very, very gentle shift, but only because I was really trying to tune in.

Then I decided to change the Clear Quartz for two Rose Quartz crystals that I have. I taped them down, and then settled in again. This time it was a bit stronger, but still very subtle. I continued though and had a good session. I was able to do my exercises in a good relaxed state, but not as meditative as last time. The Tourmalines stay wonderful as grounding crystals. Next time I will try some Tigereye.

I think the ideal would really be to have those stretch bracelets in the crystals which work best with a person. Using the rough ones just like that is fine, but I saw that some of the movements are impossible to do.

I ask myself whether there is a difference in using tumbled crystals to using the rough ones, as with the Tourmalines and Petalites."

Session 4:

"I am just continuing with what I have and in the way the crystals will tell me. I have some Golden Obsidian which I would like to try tomorrow. I also have Golden Sheen Obsidian, and I will see how I will work with them.

I asked about the experience with the transparent Quartz and did a measure with my pendulum of the effect of different crystals on my body. The result is quite interesting because normally I am very sensitive to being around transparent Quartz. But, on my body, it does not affect me in the same way.

Asking for an indication between 1 and 10 of the beneficial effect of a crystal on my body and mind during a Yoga session, I got the following results for the higher chakras:

Quartz 6
Rose Quartz 7
Amethyst 7
Petalite 9
Golden Obsidian 9
Citrine 9
Lapis 9
Kunzite 9
Moldavite 10
Emerald 10

Those last two really surprised me. I measured those because they are the crystals I can work with in the here and now. It is clear that any crystal is beneficial, but some are more helpful than others."

Session 5:

"Today I did another interesting session with them. Because I need to really take specific intentional time with them, I do not do this every day because life sometimes gets a bit busy. But today I had the occasion. My intention was to work with the Golden Sheen Obsidian for grounding and the Golden Obsidian on my wrists for higher contact. {I found this new Obsidian in South Africa last year}

I did my usual thing of placing the Generator Citrine crystal, the candle and incense. I fastened the two balls of Golden Sheen Obsidian on my feet and the Golden Obsidian on my wrists. I then slipped into a meditative state quite easily. In fact, I went rather deep, suddenly accessing some visions. This was very unexpected. One vision was a kind of long thin cross, which spins and moves, giving out an emerald green vibration.

As for the Yoga, I could center myself when I took away my meditative attention. I was very relaxed and could follow my movements. But with the standing poses it was not as easy to keep my balance when it came to doing, e.g. The Eagle position. Because I was experimenting, I then changed the Obsidian with Black Tourmaline and this was beneficial. I felt more anchored and the standing poses became easier to do. I guess to know the best grounding mineral is SO important.

That was the main objective during this session. However, I also wanted to try the energy of Moldavite and, because I was well concentrated, I used my little wand on the left-side wrist because it is the receiving side. I asked whether one could use crystals only on one side of the body, and they {the Crystal Angels} said, "No." The balance would not be good. But, I did try the Moldavite during the relaxing afterwards with the Tourmalines. It is a very special energy; quite different to the Golden Obsidian, with the energy being very fast, as well, and with other color and images following. I most definitely will be getting some other Moldavite for future use.

At this stage, I can really say, again, that any crystal, which is clean and charged properly, will be of positive help during Yoga. But it is quite important to know the grounding stone that is best for you. Those bracelets will work magic. When I am in South Africa I will be getting some at a shop I know over there. I saw them last year and they had a great choice of stones."

Helena is continuing to explore the benefit of utilizing crystals within Yoga sessions, and she will keep me updated on any new discoveries that she makes.

My daughter-in-law, Nicole, has also, on occasion, brought crystals into the area where she is performing the Yoga exercises. She has indicated that they do appear to help her achieve a greater sense of peace and balance during a session. Therefore, from both Helena's and Nicole's feedback it would seem that the mineral kingdom does impact in a positive manner on the pursuit of Yoga.

*   *   *

Recommendation to Improve a Yoga Session by the Use of Crystals

- Compare your collection of crystals with the list of earthing minerals that are given in Appendix Six. If you have some of those listed, choose one that is of good size and cleanse it.
- Sit on the floor in the area/room where you will be doing the Yoga exercises and hold the chosen crystal in your hands. Keep your thoughts and body still and allow several minutes to pass so that an energy connection can be established between you and the crystal.
- Now, ask the crystal to help you remain well-grounded during the Yoga session, and then get up and place the crystal on the floor about two feet behind where you will be standing and/or sitting.
- Remain facing the crystal and looking at it for a few moments. Then close your eyes and continue to 'see' the crystal with your inner sight.
- With the power of your imagination bring a line of connecting energy from the crystal to your Root/Base Chakra. You may well feel heat, or a tingling, or some other type of sensation in the front of your body and at the level of this chakra.
- Turn around so that your back is now facing the crystal and wait until you can feel a similar sensation at the same level, but in the back of your body. The seven main chakras are located at both the front and the back of the Etheric Body. Therefore, it is more beneficial when the connection with an earthing crystal is established with both the front and back chakra sites.
- You can now begin the Yoga session.

When you have completed the exercise, pick up the crystal, give it your thanks, and then cleanse it. If you have noticed anything different about this session from those you have previously conducted without the presence of a crystal, make a note of your findings. Later, you can compare them with any future sessions that take place with or without crystalline help.

Chapter Eight

Channeling

The New Age movement has greatly encouraged an awareness of channeling, but it may have existed for many thousands of years. When someone allows an entity or the Higher Self to speak and write through that person, it is known as "channeling." Some see this form of contact as a spiritual quest, while others consider it to be a pursuit arising from Satanism. There are also certain individuals who believe it is nothing more than a charlatan practice.

In ancient times those people, who could relay the wisdoms and teachings from other realms, were considered to be prophets or seers. Some were also thought of as witches, wizards and magicians. They stood apart from the community and were looked upon with awe and fear. However, their channeled knowledge was sometimes sought and any guidance given was deemed to be of value.

The first half of the 19th century is the time frame when our modern-day interest in channeling began. At that time it was called "spiritualism." People's attention was being propelled in new directions and their curiosity ranged beyond the 'here and now.' In 1848 the American sisters, Margaret and Kate Fox, were professing to be making contact with a spirit by means of the knocking sounds in their home. However, in later years this was known to be a fraudulent claim. By the 1870s Helena Petrovna Blavatsky was sharing channeled information which was purportedly given to her by certain mahatmas/masters. Similarly, Alice Bailey gave us the teachings of a Tibetan master in the 1920s. Also, during the first half of the 20th century, Edgar Cayce/The Sleeping Prophet was conducting channeled readings while in a deep trance state. Such people were known as "clairvoyants" and their expertise was sought in certain circles.

The 1960s, 1970s and 1980s fostered a much deeper interest in metaphysical matters. The channeled messages given to Jane Roberts by Seth, J.Z. Knight's Ramtha teachings and Shirley MacLaine's book *Out On A Limb* each made us aware of the unseen levels of existence. During the past twenty years quite a number of people have attempted various forms of channeling. For some of them it has proved to be possible, but for others it has not.

There are several methods used in order to channel. One is voice channeling in which the person passes into a trance state, and then speaks the words of an entity that has taken possession of the person's consciousness. A second way is automatic writing. The person is not in a trance, but is very relaxed and sits with eyes closed while holding a pen/pencil over a sheet of paper. Her/his hand is then guided to write without any conscious effort being made to form the words in the mind and on the paper. A variation of this method is to sit at a computer keyboard. It is also considered possible to channel works of music, paintings, poems and even entire books.

In my opinion, channeling is equally taking place within Divination. The use of the Tarot, the Runes and pendulums is tapping into, or calling upon, the vast knowledge of the Higher Self. In addition, the Ouija Board is definitely a tool for channeling, but one that should be used with caution, as should trance/voice channeling. In fact, when we allow another entity to speak, write, or relay information through us by any means, we should always be mindful of possible problems. We are opening up to other levels of existence and must guard against an intrusion by a being that is not of the very highest energy vibration.

As I explained in the Prologue, my own experience of channeling through automatic writing began in 1984. In my first non-fiction book *Soul Wisdom, Volume One*, I tell the reader how I became aware of this form of spirit communication. I tried to do automatic writing for the sole purpose of proving it was not possible. Yet my very first attempt was successful, much to my surprise. The book also documents a great deal of the fascinating information I have been given over the ensuing sessions.

Within the first few years of channeling and even though I was instructed to learn about crystals, it did not occur to me that the mineral kingdom could be incorporated into the automatic writing. It was not until 1987, when I attended a two-day seminar given by Randall N. Baer in Salem, Massachusetts, that I learned how crystals could enhance channeling. Before this man's abandonment of New Age practices and his untimely death, his work and study of the mineral kingdom was extensive. His books about crystals, e.g. *The Crystal Connection*, give unprecedented insights into the power of minerals.

Over the two-day program Randall Baer informed the attending seminar audience of his various explorations and discoveries while working closely with crystals. He particularly emphasized the need to keep them in very close proximity to the body, describing at length how he had taped various stones to his forehead for long periods of time. In this way a person could learn more about their properties.

For me the seminar was a not-to-be-missed experience with a number of unusual happenings taking place. I was very interested when Randall Baer recommended the use of Moldavite together with a Baby Herkimer Diamond as powerful aides for channeling. Moldavite is a translucent green stone that is actually a tektite, which means it is a type of meteor that fell to Earth. Originally found in the region of the Moldau River in the former Czechoslovakia, it is rare and highly prized among crystal collectors. Herkimer Diamonds are members of the Quartz Family and are not actual diamonds. First discovered in Herkimer County, N. Y. they are a type of Clear Quartz crystal that has pristine clarity and they are multi-faceted, hence their association with diamonds. They can range in size and larger specimens do exist, but the small crystals, often called "Baby Herks," are far more abundant.

At the end of the seminar I purchased a few Clear Quartz crystals and a Baby Herkimer Diamond directly from Randall Baer. I bought the later crystal because, already having a piece of Moldavite, I wanted to experiment within my channeling sessions with his suggested mineral helpers. The Moldavite specimen had come into my possession about a year earlier when I visited the "Heaven and Earth" crystal store in Gloucester, Massachusetts. This emporium of beautiful crystals and mineral specimens was run by Robert Simmons and Kathy Warner. While there I was invited by Robert Simmons to hold a piece of Moldavite, and then to give him feedback on what I felt, 'saw,' or experienced. At that early time in my association with crystals, the green tektite was unknown to me. Therefore, Robert's invitation was a golden opportunity for me to become acquainted with its awesome power.

After holding the piece for a few minutes, I told him I believed Moldavite to be a very high vibrational stone and one with which I could definitely work. He then explained that he always invited customers to hold a piece of Moldavite because he was anxious to learn more about it. Robert added that for many its energy appeared to be too strong. They either quickly felt dizzy or rapidly developed a headache. I assured him I had not felt any ill effects and I purchased the piece I was holding and a small Clear Quartz pendant with a Moldavite stone setting. In 1988 Robert Simmons and Kathy Warner published their book *Moldavite: Starborn Stone of Transformation*. I would recommend this non-fiction work to anyone who is interested in learning more about that amazing green tektite.

On returning home after the seminar, I gave some thought to how I could maintain bodily contact with the Moldavite piece and the Baby Herkimer while I was conducting automatic writing. Taping them to my forehead did not appeal to me, but I had a small crocheted pouch that my friend, Diane Stein, had previously sent to me and I decided to use that. The next time I was channeling, I put the two 'helpers' inside the pouch and placed it around my neck by means of its long cord. And this is the manner in which I have always incorporated the Moldavite and Baby Herkimer into my channeling since that time.

Do I think they have helped my contact with other levels through automatic writing? There was no sudden upswing in the intensity of the channeling, but I do believe it was enhanced by bringing them into the sessions. Looking back, I have realized that other spirit guides did not write through me before I placed the pouch around my neck. Prior to that time, the entity known to me as "Moon" was the only one who was giving me spiritual messages. Also, it did not occur to me to try voice channeling until the Moldavite and Baby Herk were resting against my chest. So perhaps crystalline enhancement within channeling broadens the scope of what can be achieved?

If you are interested in attempting some form of channeling, I would suggest you try automatic writing. As noted above, trance/voice channeling and the use of the Ouija Board need to be approached with caution and, therefore, are not advisable for the novice. Also, channeling must only be conducted within a sincere frame-of-mind and should not be considered as a fun activity or allowed to dominate your everyday life. In the Appendices of *Soul Wisdom, Volume One* I list a number of "Helpful Hints for Conducting Automatic Writing." Here are some of them:

DO:

- Meditate for at least 10 minutes before beginning.
- Ensure that you are well-grounded, centered and protected.
- Find a quiet place where you will not be disturbed.
- Burn incense and light a candle to relax yourself and to set the scene.[1]

DON'T:

- Continue if messages are blasphemous, threatening, frightening or inappropriate in any way.
- Channel if you are tired or unwell.
- Attempt to channel in a place with which you are not familiar and comfortable.
- Drink alcohol and/or take any drug {prescription or recreational} before channeling.[2]

The following exercise should set the reader on a path of exploring automatic writing. It is one that can be repeated on days when other pressing matters will not intrude upon any endeavors to make contact with the unseen realms of existence.

*   *   *

Exercise for Conducting Automatic Writing

- Choose a cleansed crystal/crystal skull that you know has earthing and protective properties, and then take a few moments to ask it to keep you safe from harm while you are open to other dimensions.
- Place the crystal/crystal skull close by where you will be sitting.
- Gather together several sheets of notepaper and pens or pencils. Have at least a couple of each writing tool in the event the pencil's lead breaks or the pen runs dry.
- Sit down at a table on a chair that gives support to your back. **N. B.** It is always important to keep the spine straight when performing this type of exercise.

- Put the notepapers and pens/pencils on the table in front of you and sit back with eyes closed.
- If you already practice meditation, allow at least 10 minutes to pass while you are in a meditative state.
- If you are not familiar with meditation, take at least 10 minutes to breathe deeply and become relaxed, dismissing any 'chatter' that your mind may try to force upon you.
- Open your eyes and put one sheet of notepaper in front of you.
- Hold either a pen or pencil in your hand and just rest the tip on the paper, as you would if you were about to begin writing.
- Close your eyes and keep your hand in this ready-to-write position.
- Ask that only the spirits from the higher realms communicate with you through automatic writing and just sit still, relaxed and waiting.
- After a few minutes you should feel your hand begin to move the pen/pencil across the notepaper.
- Do not open your eyes. Let your hand move by itself without you guiding it.
- However, if you become aware that you have moved off the paper, just open your eyes long enough to reposition the pen/pencil back in place.
- When your hand becomes still you can open your eyes and look at what has been transcribed.
- If you want to make further attempts, use another sheet of paper, making sure you keep your eyes closed once the pen/pencil is positioned on the new piece of notepaper.
- Do not pursue the automatic writing for more than about 20 minutes on this first attempt.
- On completion, express your gratitude to the unseen spirits for their contact and also thank and cleanse the crystal/crystal skull.

What can you expect to see on the notepaper? The most likely result is lines and lines of illegible scrawl that cross over each other and that have no breaks or spaces between the squiggles. However, close examination might reveal the odd word or two within the lines. Do not be discouraged if nothing is discernable on this first attempt. Try to repeat the exercise on other days, and then more and more words should become apparent. Keep trying and the indecipherable notations will become lines of words that carry messages for you. Of course, you might be fortunate enough to discover a legible communication the very first time you attempt automatic writing. It is also possible that you may see a definite, but primitive-type drawing or illustration on the paper.

Finally, whether contact appears to be made quickly or more slowly, after several sessions ask to be told with whom you are communicating and you should be given the name of the spirit who is writing through you.

1. Marion Webb-De Sisto, *Soul Wisdom, Volume One*, p. 217.
2. *Ibid.*, p. 218.

Chapter Nine

Crystal Mandalas and Grid Works

Mandalas are among the most ancient of art forms to be found in rock carvings from many parts of our world. Their circular form and variations, e.g. spirals, crosses, concentric circles, are thought to express the admiration of early human beings for the cycles of nature, the sun and moon phases/the cycle of day becoming night and the progression of the seasons. The circle also symbolized many creation myths. The Egyptians saw the cosmos as a complete circle that contained Nut, the goddess of the sky, and Geb, the god of the earth, who were bound tightly to each other. It was only when they separated, when the circle they formed was broken, that time and all life was set in motion.

Similarly, the people of Africa, India and the South Pacific considered a circular shape to be indicative of the beginning of existence. Consequently, the circle took on the role of sacred geometry, as did such things as dividing its area, calculating a right angle and defining triangular sides. In turn, these concepts were employed when building pyramids, monasteries, cathedrals and even towns. The architects were bringing the divine mathematical equations down and into an earthly level.

In India the word "mandala" was the term given to a collection of mantras/hymns that were chanted in rounds within Verdic ceremonies. The sacred sounds of these mantras gave birth to the universe and the pattern of everything within it. Once again, this displayed the belief that a circle, a round shape, signified something sacred becoming mundane. The root word "manda" means essence and the suffix "la" means container. Therefore, a mandala can be considered as a container of essence. Within the Buddhist religion it holds the presence of the Buddha inside it.

Stone circles, such as Stonehenge, can be seen as mandalas. Several years ago I stood in the center of the wide circle of stones known as The Ring of Brogar in the Orkneys. Words cannot fully explain the impact of the energy that I felt while standing there. It was like being taken to another dimension that was filled with pure stillness while a great turmoil roared outside of it.

With the passage of time the sacredness of such geometry was lost to many and today the modern world merely views its formulae as basic education. However, the circle continues to be used by some in the pursuit of sacred experiences. A circle can be cast in order for a person to feel safe while attempting to achieve the trance state, meditation, or when performing a spell or ritual. Dervishes spin to achieve a state of trance and the Plains Indians slowly spin in a circle around a pole while suspended from ropes during the sacred Sun Dance ceremony. Such people continue to believe that a mandala can change the ordinary into a sacred space, that by defining it in drawings and the arrangement of objects into a circular shape they are performing a sacred action.

The term "grid works" is normally used in connection with such things as electricity, but in this book it refers to the lines of energy that pass between minerals. The majority of people cannot see these lines, but perhaps it will be helpful to equate them with laser beams that crisscross a room as protection for something of value that is kept there. Those beams are invisible, yet they definitely exist. Similarly, the energy lines between crystals are present even though they are not visible. I have, on occasion, seen such a line emitting from a crystal point. My inner eye sees it as being very pale blue in color. However, I have never viewed a whole latticework of these lines, as one of my Elestial Reiki students once described to me. On his first visit to my home he quickly commented on how many crystals were there and that he could see all the lines of energy that were passing between them. He described a grid work of many different colors and said it was very beautiful. I certainly wished I possessed his inner visual strength because the expression on his face was one of wonder.

It is possible that these grid works exist between minerals no matter how far apart they may be positioned, but for the purpose of this chapter I am pinpointing the lines that emit from those crystals and/or crystal skulls which are within a narrow distance of each other. If they are placed into a definite pattern for whatever purpose, a network of crystalline energy lines, or channels, is also set up; and I believe this resulting grid work has greater strength due to the proximity of the minerals and the intention of creating it. The shape that the minerals form can be whatever a person feels inclined to make, but if it should be a mandala or any of its variations, then the concept of sacred geometry is being brought into play and this increases the power and higher vibration of the pattern.

As I demonstrate in Appendix Nine, etheric structures come into being when physical crystals are positioned to form certain shapes. That fact holds true no matter whether a square, a circle, a Star of David, or a completely random pattern is created. This is because crystalline energy works in tandem and just as well, if not even more proficiently, at the Etheric Level as it does at the Physical Level. This also means that the pattern's accompanying grid work is repeated etherically. Therefore, forming mandalas and any type of pattern with the help of minerals should never be undertaken lightly or without due consideration. The physical crystalline shape should not be left intact for long periods of time. This will reinforce the strength of the etheric pattern/structure, making it impossible to remove should the need arise sometime later.

A newly acquired crystal or crystal skull can be placed in the center of a circle of other previously cleansed crystals/crystal skulls in order to cleanse it. There is further information on this in Appendix Four. This crystalline mandala is giving added divinity to the newcomer as the grid work from the surrounding crystals/crystal skulls connects with it.

A mandala or other pattern can also be constructed from mineral specimens with the intention of bringing about a positive outcome, e.g. if you are trying to quit smoking, want to conquer a definite fear, or are looking for an improvement in your spiritual development. If giving distant healing to someone is something you wish to achieve, placing a 'witness' {a photograph, a lock of hair} of that person inside a mandala of crystals can help achieve this goal. Please note, it is never appropriate to give healing to another without her/his consent. You would be enforcing your own will over that of another.

There are many different things that can be accomplished by the use of crystalline mandalas, patterns and grid works. They are far too numerous to mention here and there is always room for more. So be creative, but always remember that you are tapping into an awesome energy, which some might consider pure magic. Be responsible with and respectful of that power and never employ it with anything other than the highest and purest of intentions.

*   *   *

Exercise to Create a Crystalline Mandala

You will need to find a suitable location for your mandala. This should be somewhere in your home that is away from the everyday traffic of family, friends and pets, e.g. a bedroom, an unused room, a quiet corner of a study, hallway, or landing. The mandala can be constructed on a small table, the top of a bookcase or bureau, a non-cluttered area of the floor, or anywhere that you feel is appropriate. Before construction, you should have some of your collection of mineral specimens at hand. These can be crystals that are in the rough or have been carved and polished, crystal clusters, crystal skulls, spheres, obelisks, etc. All of these should be already cleansed.

- Take your mineral collection to the place you have chosen to be the location of your mandala.
- Sit down close by, close your eyes and begin to relax by breathing deeply and putting aside any thoughts that are not connected to what you are about to do.
- Affirm that you want to construct a mandala that will help clarify your soul purpose for being incarnated at this time. {None of us are here by accident; we each have a role to fulfill.}
- Open your eyes and 'go with the flow.' Whichever mineral specimens of your collection seem to be the correct ones to use are the right crystals. Place them, one at a time, in whatever pattern you feel drawn to make. Your choices and the mandala shape are being guided by the higher realms.
- You will most probably only use some of the specimens from your collection, but that is as it should be. You will be given guidance about when to stop constructing the mandala.
- Take a few minutes to become familiar with your creation. Is the shape different from what you expected? Have your choices of mineral specimens surprised you? Can you 'see' the grid work that has formed between the crystals? During this time you will also be building a connection with your mandala.
- It can also be useful to jot down the formed pattern on paper as a reminder of how it appears.

- Thank the higher realms for helping you and leave the mandala untouched and undisturbed for 24 hours. During that time the etheric double of your mandala and its grid work are being imprinted.
- Once the time period has elapsed, disassemble the mandala, cleanse and thank the mineral specimens and return them to their usual 'home.'

With this particular exercise it is not necessary to remove the etheric mandala at some future date because it pertains to an ongoing aspect of your life. However, if you do feel the need to remove it later on, follow these instructions:

- If you made a sketch of your mandala, take it with you to the place where the physical crystalline pattern was formed. If you did not or you no longer have the paper, just close your eyes and try to recall the mandala's detail and shape. Even if you cannot, the removal will take place providing you are sincere in your approach.
- Close your eyes and imagine the etheric mandala as being above your head. Make sweeping and pushing motions with your hands, affirming that you are deconstructing its etheric substance.
- Ask that its form be sent to the higher realms and express your gratitude for its help.
- Know that your mandala continues to clarify your soul purpose from the very highest level of existence.
- Give thanks to the mineral kingdom, your spirit guides and angelic helpers and go about your daily life.

Part Three

Combining Crystals with Divination

Chapter Ten

Scrying

The art of scrying is a form of divination or clairvoyance, which is the ability to see what is hidden from our mundane lives. The word "scrying" is derived from the Anglo Saxon word "descry," which is believed to mean "reveal." Evidence of scrying within ancient cultures has been found in various places across our planet. In Egypt seers used blood, ink, or any dark liquid for divination and the Romans sought advice from shiny objects and stones. The Egyptian goddess Hathor was believed to possess a shield that was sometimes identified as a mirror. It guarded her against the evil intentions of others. Apart from reflecting back any negativity that was focused on her, it also allowed the goddess to 'see' all things in their true light. As such, it was a tool for scrying. In a similar manner the ancient Greek and Celtic populations utilized the minerals Beryl and Clear Quartz, dark glass, water and any other type of transparent and/or light-catching object. In South America Obsidian was considered beneficial when attempting to pursue such endeavors as foretelling the future, revealing secrets, or revisiting the past. Michel de Notre-dame, or Nostradamus as he is more commonly known, is believed to have used a bowl or small pail of water when divining the future. Edward Kelley, who was an assistant to the alchemist John Dee, consulted a crystal ball that can be seen on display at the British Museum in London.

Therefore, all of the examples above demonstrate the obvious fact that scrying has been a popular pursuit, reaching far back into history and, at times, incorporating the help of the mineral kingdom. Today it remains as a metaphysical discipline that fascinates people. The most common ways of employing it are by using:

Mirrors
Crystal Spheres or Crystal Skulls
Water in a Bowl, a Small Pond, or Small Pool
Tea Leaves
Coffee Grinds
Glowing Embers in a Fire
A Dimly-lit/Candle-lit Room {watching the formation of shadows or looking
into the eyes of another person who sits facing you}
The Rising Smoke from Burning Incense

When scrying, one gazes steadily into the reflective surface, the pattern
of leaves and grinds, the fire's embers, or the shifting shadows and swirling
smoke. These mediums help to focus the attention, removing any unwanted
thoughts and serving the same purpose as a mantra, when attempting
meditation. If using a reflective surface, including a crystal sphere or crystal
skull, a mist/cloud will usually appear after a short while of gazing at the
scrying object. The mist/cloud may change color and this is interpreted by
some as having meaning, e.g. white for positive outcomes, green for acquiring
money and/or a good relationship with someone. It may also rise or fall in
answer to direct questions. A rising mist/cloud is considered to mean "Yes" and
a falling one should be interpreted as "No." Eventually, images and symbols
may then become apparent within it.

The patterns that tea leaves and coffee grinds display in the bottom of
cups are the indicators of hidden messages. Similarly, the forms that take
shape within the rising smoke and glowing embers, and the shadows that
cast silhouettes in a darkened room, can be interpreted by the person who is
performing the scrying act.

Images that are seen within any type of scrying medium might be very
crude in structure, but they can also be quite detailed. They may be as
clear as when looking at a photograph or picture. However, when a person
first attempts scrying it is far more common for her/him to experience
vague and sporadic shapes and symbols. This can create difficulties in
interpreting what is being seen. There is no accompanying booklet, as
with the Tarot and Runes, which will help decipher the meanings for the
person who is scrying. Accomplished Tarot and Rune readers invariably
rely on their own psychic ability, when understanding the messages of the
cards and stones that have been chosen. They made use of the booklets
in the beginning, but now have confidence in whatever they feel their

clairvoyant skills are presenting to them. Scrying requires the same level of inner assurance that what is being interpreted is correct. Therefore, scrying requires patience, repeated practice and a belief in one's aptitude for understanding the meaning of the apparent shapes, images and symbols that are visible within the scrying tool. However, I do believe that when crystalline power is utilized, i.e. scrying with a crystal sphere or crystal skull, the interpretations are more easily accessed.

Scrying is not a form of divination that I have personally followed while attempting to gain answers to questions and/or seeking hidden truths. This is probably because I have a preference for consulting the Runes. However, I am aware that many people, who practice this form of divination, do so with the help of the mineral kingdom, and this, once again, demonstrates how minerals aid and work well with yet another metaphysical pursuit.

Even though I am not actively involved in the art of scrying, this does not mean that I consider it to be a lesser medium. Each one of us is unique and different, and what appeals to one person may not be appropriate for another. Therefore, I am offering information on scrying here so that if the reader does feel inclined to explore this divining tool, s/he will have a basic understanding of it. The following exercise should prove helpful to anyone who feels drawn to this fascinating form of divination and, as with other disciplines put forward in this book, it involves the use of minerals.

*　　*　　*

Scrying Exercise with a Crystal Sphere or Crystal Skull

Choose a sphere that has a diameter of at least 3" or a skull that measures not less than 3" from front to back. Either one can have been carved from Clear Quartz, Citrine, or Obsidian and should be cleansed prior to use. Also have ready a candle and incense, and then locate a room or area that is away from a window and direct sunlight. The reflections of light on the crystal can distract the attention from the purpose of the exercise. Choose a chair/seat close to a table and where the spine will remain in a straight position. Begin by:

- Placing the candle, incense and crystal sphere/crystal skull on the table. If using a sphere, then a stand will be needed so that the crystal does not roll. If using a skull, the face should be turned away from the person, who is scrying, so that the cranium can be observed.

- Sit down in front of the table and light the candle and incense, making sure the candlelight is not reflecting on the crystal's surface.
- Take several minutes to relax and affirm the intention of scrying.
- The help of personal spirit guides and angelic helpers can also be called upon.
- Now focus the gaze right into the center of the crystal rather than merely looking at its surface.
- After a few minutes a mist/cloud should appear within the depth of the crystal.
- If "Yes" and "No" answers are being sought to specific questions, ask each one at a time. Take note of whether the mist/cloud rises or falls in response.
- Also note whether it changes color, and then wait to be given a sense of what the coloration changes mean.
- If scrying is being pursued in order to be shown shapes and symbols, continue to gaze at the mist/cloud until a clearing takes place. Then vague or more distinct images should appear.
- Remain watching what is being shown and try to ascertain the meaning of the display.
- When nothing more is being given, remove the focus from the crystal and take a few moments to stretch and bring your full awareness back to mundane life.
- Extinguish the candle and incense and give thanks to the mineral kingdom and the spirit realms for the assistance that was received during the scrying session.
- Cleanse the crystal sphere/crystal skull and position back in its usual 'home.'

Be prepared for no images to be seen on the first attempt. Even the mist/cloud may not change color or move up and down, but do not be discouraged. Success within scrying may take a number of sessions before it is achieved. Remember the saying that "practice makes perfect." If, however, nothing is being gleaned from many attempts, then it is possible that a different form of divination is more appropriate. The following three chapters may just be the ones that offer successful alternatives.

Chapter Eleven

The Tarot

There are many fascinating stories about how the Tarot cards came into existence. Some speculate they originated in ancient Egypt, others believe the Gypsies/Traveling People first brought them to Europe hundreds of years ago. Another theory claims a group of Moroccan intellectuals created them to preserve their ancient wisdom in the form of pictures. The cards' origin is even claimed by some to be extraterrestrial. Whatever is true or false about these theories has only added to the popularity of the Tarot.

It is known that a deck of cards for a game called "Tarocco" was made for the Vicsconzi-Sforza family of Milan in the late 14th century. It became a popular pastime of the nobility of Italy to play this card game, and it also spread eventually to France. Some three hundred years later, the speculation that the cards represented great symbolism began to be accepted. This happened when a certain individual named De Geblen saw the game being played with a set of Marseilles cards that had evolved from the Vicsconzi-Sforza deck. Soon the idea that the Tarocco cards were a divination tool spread and another man, Alliette, helped to cement this belief into the mind of the general public. By the late 1800s, *The Tarot of the Bohemians* had been published and the Tarot was here to stay. This was also the time when the Hermetic Order of the Golden Dawn came into existence.

It was a tradition within the Golden Dawn that its members had to create their own Tarot cards. The decks of two members, Aleister Crowley and Arthur Edward Waite, have become well-known to many. Crowley's deck is *The Book of Thoth* and Waite's cards are the popular *Rider Waite Tarot*.

Both decks are filled with symbolism, but Crowley's is considered to be more in-depth and complex. I have my own deck of The Book of Thoth, purchased some years ago in Salem, Massachusetts, and I can attest to its multifaceted symbolism.

In the early 19th century, Eliphas Levi correlated the similarity of the Tarot with occult traditions, the Hebrew system of mysticism and the Kabbalah. De Geblen had also noted that there were 22 trump cards and 22 letters in the Hebrew alphabet. However, Levi tied the Tarot into the Tree of Life and considered the cards to be essential for a human being to develop herself/himself. The Tarot was a tool to achieve enlightenment.

Throughout the 20th century a number of different Tarot decks became available to buy. Many are a conglomeration or variation of the Crowley and Waite cards. If the reader feels drawn to the Tarot, I would advise her/him to examine different decks, and then work with the one with which s/he feels comfortable.

An English woman who has closely studied the Tarot is Sue Bouvier. She holds a certificate in BAPS-Tarot, is a qualified Crystal Healing practitioner and is also a Druid priestess. I first met Sue in 2001 when she attended one of my workshops on crystal skulls. Her interest in these wonderful mineral carvings is documented in my book *Crystal Skulls*.

Sue's love of the mineral kingdom and the Tarot has led her to focus on bringing crystals into readings to, as she explained, "strengthen the read of the card." She has also established a further link between the Tarot and the mineral kingdom by using crystals in place of cards, relying on her own "intuition and feelings of the crystals." Having studied both Cassandra Eason's and Scott Cunningham's Crystal Major Arcana Tarots, Sue has created a part of her own Crystal Tarot. This exercise in substitution is an on-going project and Sue recognizes that equating a crystal with each of the Major and Minor Arcana cards will take a great deal of time for someone who is pursuing several studies and working full time. However, I believe what she has already formulated through meditation and her knowledge of the Tarot and crystals is worthy of documentation. I offer her explanation of it below for the reader's appreciation and interest.

Sue's Personal Crystal Major Arcana Tarot

"After much meditating with many crystals and their vibration/energies, I list below my initial Crystal Tarot, my reasons for the choice of each crystal to represent each Major Arcana card and its path through the journey of life. I have also only given a brief outline of what each Major Arcana card represents to me. The Tarot is such a wide divination tool and I have many different Tarot decks, all being used for different types of reads. I chose my Old Path deck to help me create this particular Crystal Tarot.

I have not given any examples of other crystals I tried, having decided against this because it would take up too much room. So I have listed my final choices at this stage of my experiment.

The Fool—Topaz

The Fool is about to start off on his new journey. He is carefree and a little irresponsible, so my choice of Topaz was because it represents to me the charisma and self-confidence he will need as he commences his journey. But it also represents reality and this is a quality he will need in order to keep himself on his new path. It will help develop his plans and ideas as he moves along his path.

The Magician—Labradorite

As The Fool moves along his path and gains experience, he becomes The Magician—the man of many skills. He is now the young pupil who is learning to use what knowledge he has to enable him to move on along his path. So I chose Labradorite because to me it not only represents masculine magic {and The Magician is magical} and helping to develop intuition, but it also helps develop new ideas and new skills that are at a 'young' stage. It is a crystal that also brings back forgotten memories; and so, The Magician is able to use skills he has used before, as well as new skills to help him grow.

The High Priestess—Lapis Lazuli

The High Priestess is the card of deep intuition and gut feelings that guide our inner consciousness. Lapis Lazuli to me is an ancient magical crystal, which gives wisdom and honesty, and enables us to help others, as well as ourselves. The High Priestess shows us how to use our inner resources, and Lapis Lazuli represents this aspect of ourselves.

The Empress—Moonstone

The Empress is the mother in us all and the mother we look to when we are down and things are not going right. Moonstone is a feminine crystal of magic and mystery, but also a gentle loving and caring crystal and, I felt, absolutely represents the gentle feminine qualities of The Empress.

The Emperor—Jade

The Emperor is the solid institution of the Tarot. He has his roots very firmly planted in the material world; and so I chose Jade to represent these qualities. Jade to me represents balance and self-realization, showing that although it is a grounder, it also helps us to face the fact that not everything is rooted in the material world, but that spirituality needs to be remembered.

The Hierophant—Copper

The Hierophant is locked in strong ideas and is, again, rooted in the real material world. But he is a man of commitment; and so I felt that Copper was the right crystal to represent him. Copper is solid, grounding and focused.

The Lovers—Malachite

The Lovers are seen by many people as two people in love, but in actuality it is a card of choice, the selection of a partner, a job, a place to live, or a new direction. It is about making the right choice to enable the journeyer to move forward. Malachite to me feels so right here. It is a crystal of friendship, empathy, dreams and imagination. It awakens the desire for knowledge, which is needed if the right choice is to be made. It is a crystal that helps with desires and looking at desires in a rational way. It dissolves pain, and that is needed if the choice is a difficult one.

The Chariot—Peridot

The Chariot is the card of finding strength now that the direction indicated by The Lovers has been chosen. It is about taking control to implement that new choice. Peridot helps to detach from outside influences and so use our own resources to live our own life and draw on our inner knowledge. It also dissolves feelings that we cannot take control of ourselves.

Strength—Kyanite

This card shows that the journeyer has now found the inner strength to continue to move along his path. It can also show reconciliation between two people who have fallen out. Kyanite to me is a steely strong crystal that particularly helps the emotional bodies. It helps us look objectively at ourselves, overriding negativity and feelings that we are not strong and/or cannot deal with problems. It encourages rationality, which is now needed at this stage in the journey.

The Hermit—Pyrite

The Hermit represents the period we all have to go through of feeling very much alone on our particular path. He has wisdom and knowledge acquired both along the way and in past lives, but at this stage cannot see quite where to go next. He is introvert and feels very much alone, and is only able to take one small step at a time. However, that step is along the right path, and deep within himself he knows this. But he feels very isolated and lonely. Pyrite encourages us to accept ourselves as we are and to accept that we do have the knowledge we need. It shows us who we are at this particular stage. It brings out our innermost secrets to enable us to become open and not to hold back any longer, but to slowly move along the path, knowing that we are going in the right direction.

The Wheel of Fortune—Tigereye

The Wheel of Fortune is the ups and downs of life and life's problems. It shows us that everything goes round in a circle and what is bad now will, again, become good. It warns us that, of course, what is good now can become bad if we do not make the right choices or do the right things. Tigereye helps give courage and the acceptance that things will become right, again, or that anything bad can be put right. It helps us stand back and view life in an unemotional way and it helps dissolve pain, too. It helps us remove doubt and stress from our life. And it also keeps us grounded.

Justice—Sugilite

Justice is the card of "what goes round comes round." It is the card of Karma. What is given out will be repaid and what is taken must be put back. And, of course, it is the card of legal dealings. Whether you win or lose will depend entirely on what you did or did not do correctly. Sugilite helps us stand by our own point-of-view and to come to decisions based on our inner truths. It helps us deal with unpleasantness and to overcome conflict. To me, Sugilite is very much a crystal of justice, whether helping us to stand by our rightful decisions or to face up to something we know is wrong.

The Hanged Man—Bloodstone

The Hanged Man is the centre of the journey, where we have to wait for a while whilst we decide whether to continue or not, and whilst we absorb what has been learnt so far. It is the card of isolation and meditation. It is the card of the chrysalis that will become the butterfly, but only when the time is right. It can be a card of stagnation so, to me, Bloodstone helps to open doors and calm fears that are holding The Hanged Man back from moving on.

Death—Black Tourmaline

The Death card is where, in order to move on our journey, something in our past and present must be swept aside. The dead wood in our life must be cut away so that the path becomes clear enough for us to walk along. Black Tourmaline is a strong 'letting go' crystal. It indicates that letting go is important before we can move on. It will help remove the dead wood and will also act to protect us during this process. It will help us to accept that once we have let go, we can move on. It is a strong negativity-removing crystal and this, to me, is what the Death card of the Tarot represents.

Temperance—Blue Lace Agate

Temperance, to me, represents that despite the previous card having removed the dead wood from our lives, there is a problem in our life that has resurfaced. And this needs to be dealt with, but it needs to be dealt with in a gentle way. The removal of the dead wood by the Death card has left us feeling a little vulnerable, and when this old problem resurfaces, we wonder if we are going to be able to handle it. But we are, and there is much positivity around this card of Temperance. Blue Lace Agate is a gentle crystal; and so it represents the gentleness needed to deal with stress, and to calm us down into a more relaxed state in order to deal with the problem.

The Devil—Red Jasper

The Devil is the card of negativity, greed, thinking of only ourselves and not being bothered whether someone else gets hurt or not. Red Jasper is a good representation of The Devil in that its deep color is the color often associated with the devil and so immediately makes us think of the devil and what he represents. But this crystal will help to ground us in our Base Chakra; and so face our own greed and nastiness. Also, it will send back any negativity around us to where it came from.

The Tower—Smoky Quartz

The Tower is the collapse of our life so that a new part of our life can be rebuilt. As new buildings grow from destroyed foundations, so will our life. But it is a card of shock and, therefore, I feel needs a strong crystal to represent it. Smoky Quartz to me feels right because it is a strong crystal and, of course, the new structure in our life will need to be strong, as we also need the strength to overcome this disastrous time and to cope with difficulties, both as The Tower collapses and as the new building starts to emerge. Smoky Quartz helps to separate thoughts, feelings and deep inner fears, and to strengthen resolve.

The Star—Apophyllite

The Star is the card of hope. Of little things coming in to help us and to bring us pleasure. There is only one crystal that to me represents The Star and that is Apophyllite. It has a bright happy energy and brings joy and excitement. To me it is totally The Star Tarot card of the crystal kingdom.

The Moon—Black Obsidian

The Moon represents the dark side. Illusion and things not being what they appear. It is the card of despair and negativity so to represent this I chose

Black Obsidian. In its polished form it is deep black, but there is quite often sheen on it, so it does not look as black as it is. This to me represents the illusion of The Moon as it brings deep hidden issues to light from within the unconscious mind; and so helps us face up to the reality of the illusion.

The Sun—Amber

The Sun represents the happiness now gained by dealing with all the obstacles and tests along the journey path; and so, to me, Amber feels so right to represent The Sun. Amber looks like sunshine and the energy is that of self-confidence, spontaneity, freedom and happiness. It is creative and dissolves any feelings of low self-esteem. It is The Sun.

Judgment—Hawk's Eye

Judgment is the card of new beginnings. The end of the journey has almost been reached and the old way has been left behind. It is now time to start a new phase of life. Hawk's Eye helps you to accept your own responsibility and not to lay the blame on others.

The World—Amethyst

The World is the final completion of the journey. All skills needed along the journey have been learnt and now is the time to say, "Goodbye" to the old way and look forward to the new. It is often a spiritual card, too, showing not only physical travel but also spiritual travel. To me Amethyst has awoken and taken us to higher spiritual levels; and so allows us to travel further and higher on our spiritual path. In the physical world, its energies help with the inspiration to accept that the journey has completed and we can look forward to the beginning of the new journey. It has given us new experiences to allow us to move on with an excited calmness."

I am ending this chapter with an exercise that the reader may find interesting. In recent years, I have belonged to a couple of Yahoo Groups of people who collect and work with crystal skulls. On one occasion a member of one group, Jeanne Dunn, set a challenging exercise for others to attempt. It involved conducting a Tarot reading in order to become acquainted with a particular crystal skull. Using Tarot cards in connection with these mineral carvings is something with which I was already familiar. In *Crystal Skulls* I wrote about Samantha Elliott, who had conducted Tarot readings for several of my crystal friends. The insights she gave were extremely accurate even though she had not actually seen any of the skulls. Jeanne Dunn's recommendations to the group on why and how to conduct the exercise were helpful and easy to follow. For the reader, who is the custodian of a crystal skull and who is interested in attempting this exercise, her guidelines are documented below.

*   *   *

Exercise to Become Acquainted with a Crystal Skull with the Help of the Tarot

"Getting Acquainted:

A crystal skull has come into your life. It may be your first. It may be one of several, but this is a skull who presents a challenge. It is a quiet skull. A skull with whom you would like to connect, but there is no 'spark', or there is a sense that there is a chasm between you that needs crossing.

This Tarot spread may help you bridge the gap. It begins with you on one end and the crystal skull on the other. The steps in between help create a path upon which you two can meet and become acquainted.

If you are new to the Tarot, I recommend two things. Work with a traditional deck because it is more likely that others can help you with your interpretation if you do, and there is a LOT of reference material on the individual cards of a traditional deck. The second thing I recommend is to read all cards as if they are upright, even if you turn them up reversed. When you become more familiar with the intricacies of the Tarot, then you can move into interpretation of reversed cards.

Those of you who are familiar with the Tarot, of course, have the experience to work with alternative decks and understand the nuances of reversed cards, so go for it!

The Meditation:

Once you have selected the skull with which you will be doing the five-card Bridge spread, spend some time in meditation with it. We probably each have our own meditation methods, so I won't go into great detail here, but this is what works for me:

- I light some incense a few minutes prior to the meditation in order to fill the area with scent. I light a candle while doing my prayers of protection and my request for Divine guidance. For this particular meditation I will also choose to play music. I do believe that the skulls respond to sound, and I have a Native American flute CD that will be perfect because the skull with whom I will be working is Spirit Warrior. After he gave me his name, he seemed to go into quiet mode. I admire him all the time, but we have not connected on a significant level yet.
- Spend at least 15 minutes in meditative silence with your skull. Focus on the intent to connect and commune. Open yourself to the energies and spirit of the skull. Should you feel the connection begin, you should respond in an enthusiastic and grateful way/a joyful heart to encourage and maintain that connection. Enjoy that feeling for a moment, and then, when the time feels right, set your skull down facing you and work the following Tarot spread between you.

Although many of you are familiar with the Tarot, I will start with the basics for those who might not be.

- Before each reading, I go through a personal process that I call "righting the deck." I turn up each card and lay it upright in an arc, like a rainbow, on the desk in front of me. Then, with eyes closed, I pull the two ends of the arc together, gathering the deck in a pile in the center and I straighten the cards. This is a habit I got into years ago and it just feels right, making sure that all is in order prior to shuffling. **N. B.** I do not put them in order by suit or number. I just make sure they are all upright! This exercise also enables me to 'feel' the cards. I focus on my intent while doing this, too, and it really enhances concentration and connection with the cards and with Spirit.
- Once you have "righted the deck," should you even choose to do this, set the deck face down and set your skull on top of the deck. Touch the skull. Spend another moment in meditative communion with the skull, then remove the skull and begin shuffling.

- You should shuffle your deck three times, as thoroughly as you can. After the third shuffle, set your deck down to the left and cut it twice to the right so you have three piles. Pick up the left pile, set it on top of the center pile and set that on top of the last pile. You are now ready to work the spread diagrammed below. Note the numbers in the diagram.

- You do not set the cards out in straight order from left to right. It works far left, far right, near left, near right, center. The positions are to be interpreted as follows:

SPREAD: The Bridge {Five-Card Version}

1. **You:** Representing your current state of mind and circumstances right at this moment. How this affects your perception/interaction with the skull.

2. **The Skull:** What is required to establish rapport? What does the skull need from you?

3. **Challenges:** Challenges, obstacles, the things/persons that are holding you back in life and/or preventing you from connecting with this crystal skull.

4. **Lessons/Growth:** Your ability/willingness to learn from this skull—what lessons and opportunities for personal growth does s/he bring?

5. **Healing/Evolution:** What aspects of yourself/life will this crystal skull help you heal? How will s/he enhance your spiritual evolution?

The Message: After reading the individual positions of the spread, see if you can put it all together and receive the overall message that your crystal skull may be trying to relay to you."

Some of their feedback is documented in Appendix One. Almost one year later, Jeanne, again, offered the exercise for exploration, and several people participated. A couple of their comments and interpretations are also included in the same Appendix.

Chapter Twelve

The Runes

As with the history of the Tarot, there is much speculation about the origin of the Runes. However, pre-runic symbols have been found in Bronze Age rock carvings, mostly in Sweden. Some of those symbols can be identified in the alphabets of later times, but the exact meanings and primary purpose of them is lost. It is thought they may have been used for divination, and it is reasonably certain that they became part of the runic alphabets which first emerged around 200 B.C.E. These pictographic sigils appear to be a combination of the earlier symbols with some of the Greek or Latin letters. The latter alphabet seems to be the more likely choice. When the Germanic tribes integrated their pre-runic symbols with the Latin alphabet, the Runes began to spread throughout Northern and Middle Europe. Thus, a magical and talismanic system of divination was born.

The name "futhark" is derived from the first few letters of the runic alphabet which originally consisted of 24 letters. It was used by the tribes of Scandinavia and Northern Germany, and is known as the Elder or Germanic Futhark. However, by 300 A.D. it had fallen into less usage in Europe due to the expansion of Christianity and the widespread use of the Latin alphabet.

Sometime after 400 A.D., alterations were made to this runic alphabet. Extra symbols were added to accommodate changes within the language and some were given additional letters. These adjustments coincided with the Anglo-Saxon invasions, and the new Anglo-Saxon Futhorc made an appearance within the British Isles.

During the 8th century, substantial alterations occurred within the Norse language and consequently they were reflected in the runic alphabet. The original 24 letters of the Elder Futhark were reduced to 16 and the symbols were simplified. This new runic alphabet, known as the Younger Futhark, spread from Denmark to Sweden and Norway and was later carried by the Vikings into Iceland and Greenland.

The Runes were never the basis of a spoken language, but were carved into wood or stone, and were also transcribed onto other materials. They were considered sacred and to possess supernatural properties. Some were linked to certain Norse gods. They could be written from left to right or right to left; as mirror images or upside down; and even sometimes joined together. Spaces between each symbol were often indicated by one, two, or three points/dots. For example, ":" and there were no lowercase Runes.

For the next eight hundred years, the runic alphabet, usually in the form of the Younger Futhark, was in common usage as a means of divination. Rune casters, who were often women, used this alphabet to cast lots and tell fortunes. Originally, the Runes were sanctioned by the Church, but during the early 17th century, when magical arts and the like were considered to be the work of the Devil, they were banned. Those people who continued to use them were either executed or went underground. Therefore, for the next three hundred years, knowledge of the Runes was probably passed on in secret.

In the 1920s and 1930s, German scholars initiated a revival of runic interest. This began as a genuine exploration of Germanic folklore, but it soon became tainted by its association with Nazism. Consequently, for the next twenty-odd years the Runes were, once again, considered to be a part of evil pursuits. It was not until the emergence of the "New Age" ideology that they regained their former popularity as a tool for divination and self-development. This rediscovery of their worthwhile potential has continued into the present day.

I purchased my own set of Runes in the early 1980s and I have always found them to be helpful in offering answers to questions about myself and/or other matters that concern me. The only method I have ever used of incorporating the mineral kingdom into runic pursuit is to keep a small piece of rough Black Obsidian in the same pouch as my Runes. This volcanic glass is extremely protective and that is my reason for keeping it with them. It keeps at bay any untoward energy vibrations that might influence the order in which the Runes are withdrawn from the pouch. This, in turn, could alter the dynamics of the answers being given. Keeping a small piece of Black Obsidian within close proximity to any divination method, e.g. the Tarot cards, the I-Ching and the Ouija Board, will work equally as well as it does with the Runes.

It is possible to obtain crystal Runes. Sets are created from such minerals as Sugilite, Fluorite, Agate, Amethyst, Quartz and Jasper. When using Sugilite and Amethyst Runes, a person will be stimulating her/his 3rd Eye/Brow Chakra which could, in turn, help in understanding the higher truth within any spread. Brown and Red Agate Runes, as well as those created from Jasper, should prove particularly helpful in answering questions about down-to-earth matters. As explained in Appendix Six, these are earthing minerals and will emphasize the practical meaning of runic answers.

One member of a Yahoo group to which I belong told me she has a set of Runes that were carved on small pieces of Aventurine. They have been in her keeping for a number of years and she feels very relaxed when handling them. Aventurine is a crystal for the Heart Chakra and, I think, it should work in tandem with the Runes. The Heart Chakra is the bridge between the upper and lower chakras and it aids in manifesting the soul's desires into physical reality. The Runes help us understand those desires by pinpointing how we should, or should not, act in any given circumstance. In addition, they clarify the reasons behind what we experience in our day-to-day lives. Therefore, I can see a strong and viable link between runic engravings and the mineral named Aventurine.

The examples given above are just a few indicators of how crystalline energy can enhance the runic symbols, but I am in no way advocating a preference to consult those which have been etched on minerals. If you have a set, which was created from some other material and with which you are familiar and comfortable, continue to seek help and guidance from those tablets. However, if my shared information in this chapter with regard to crystalline enhancement of the Runes may have stirred your interest, then try one of the following runic exercises:

*   *   *

Runic Enhancement Suggestions

Exercise 1:

- Choose a rough or polished mineral specimen, a crystal skull, or a figure carved from a crystal, e.g. a Quan Yin, a Buddha, etc. Cleanse it and ask for its assistance in understanding whatever runic spread you place in front of you.

- Lay out the necessary number of Runes, face down on the table, or wherever you choose to work, and then turn them over in the correct order. Take time to define their runic message.
- Now, place your crystalline aid a few inches away from the chosen Runes and notice whether further meaning or a more in-depth understanding presents itself to you. If you have experienced difficulty in discerning the runic message, you may now find that it has suddenly become quite clear.
- Do not forget to cleanse the mineral specimen, once you have completed this runic exercise.

Exercise 2:

- Choose a number of cleansed Clear Quartz tumblestones. Ask for their help in clarifying whichever runic spread you will consult, and then lay them aside. Their quantity should match however many Runes are required for the chosen spread, e.g. 3, 5, or 6.
- Select the number of Runes necessary for the spread and lay them out, face down.
- Next, place one tumblestone on each of the runic tablets and leave them there, untouched, for at least ten minutes. This will allow time for the Quartz energy to permeate the Runes so that their meanings will be clarified for you.
- Now return to the spread and, one at a time, remove the Quartz tumblestone, turn over the Rune and 'read' its message.
- Cleanse the tumblestones when this runic exercise is finished.

Exercise 3:

- Choose a crystal skull, a mineral sphere, or a shaped wand and be sure that your choice is cleansed. Next, decide upon a runic symbol that you believe will be helpful to you, e.g. Algis—Protection, Wunjo—Joy, Gebo—Partnership, Uruz—Strength, etc.
- Draw or paint this symbol on a piece of paper, making its dimensions roughly the same as those of your chosen skull, sphere, or wand.
- Place your mineral friend on the paper, centering it over the symbol, and ask it to absorb the energy of this runic character. Leave this placement undisturbed for at least 24 hours.

- Once you have removed the skull, sphere, or wand, you can ask for its help during meditation, sleep, work, etc. by keeping it close to you and within your auric field. Apart from the healing properties of the mineral kingdom, you will also be receiving the blessing of whichever runic quality your crystal friend has taken into itself.

- Periodically, cleanse the chosen skull, sphere, or wand. This will not remove the specific runic energy that your crystal friend has absorbed unless you specifically ask it to do so.

- If that is your choice, then just ask for the energy pattern to disintegrate and to be gone during the cleansing process. Having done this, allow the skull, sphere, or wand to rest for a few days before working with it in any new capacity.

Chapter Thirteen

Pendulums & Dowsing

The word "dowsing" is a relatively new term used to describe a form of psychic divining, but this practice has existed for thousands of years. In the Atlas Mountains a cave painting was discovered some sixty years ago that appeared to depict a dowser holding a forked stick. This wall mural was carbon dated as being about 8,000 years old. In Egypt there are 4,000 year old etchings on temple walls of pharaohs using dowsing tools, and at least one Chinese emperor is believed to have possessed a pronged wooden device. Both Moses and Aaron used "the Rod" to locate water and there are other references within the Bible to diviners consulting pieces of wood. The Ancient Greeks were familiar with dowsing and it is thought that the Oracle of Delphi employed a pendulum in order to answer the questions put forward to her by royal rulers, the nobility and military commanders.

By the Middle Ages dowsing tools were being used by German miners to detect the locations of mineral ores. In 1650 in an essay written by the English philosopher, John Locke, the use of a "dowsing rod" was recommended as a means of discovering water and precious metals, such as gold and silver. In the 18th and 19th centuries various English, German and French books about mining and engineering referred extensively to the art of dowsing. In the present-day libraries of both Harvard and Yale there are a number of books on this particular method of divination.

What exactly is a dowsing rod? Traditionally it is a small branch with a natural fork at one end that has been cut from a willow tree. It is held out by its single end in front of a dowser who walks slowly across the area/field/locality in question. The forked ends will either begin to vibrate or even point downwards to the position of whatever is being sought. If there is no movement along the rod, then it can be concluded that the water, mineral, etc. is not present. In more recent times two rods have been employed for dowsing. These are usually straight with one angled end and made from metal. The dowser grasps the rods loosely by the angled ends, holds them out at right angles from the body and just below chest level. S/he then moves slowly over the designated area until the rods cross over each other, pinpointing the exact placement of whatever s/he is seeking. Sometimes the rods will spin rapidly round and round, like propellers, instead of crossing over.

The use of a pendulum instead of a divining rod is probably equally as ancient. Ceramic pendulums that were found in old Egyptian tombs are held in the Cairo Museum, and those made from bone and colored stones have also been discovered in different places across the planet. All of these tools should contain some type of minerals, therefore, highlighting, once again, the relationship between dowsing and the crystalline world. Just like a divining rod, a pendulum was the tool that could pinpoint a water source. It could also give "Yes" or "No" answers to questions about a compatible lover, the right time or location for planting a crop, or the gender of an unborn child. Farmers have even been known to dowse a batch of eggs with a pendulum before placing them in an incubator. In this way they can control the number of roosters by restricting those that will be allowed to hatch.

As mentioned in the above paragraph, pendulums were traditionally carved from bone or cast from some type of clay. They were suspended at the end of a thread or fine chain and held a couple of inches above whatever was in question, e.g. an egg, a map, the palm of a pregnant woman, etc. A pendulum could also be held out in front of the dowser who then watched and interpreted its movements. In today's world people use many different suspended small objects as pendulums, e.g. a fishing line sinker, a ring, an earring, a button, or a pendant. Whatever is available will work.

I have now detailed the tools for conducting dowsing, but how does it actually work? No one is absolutely certain. Perhaps it is a leftover ability that primitive man needed to ensure that he could find water, food and shelter? Or maybe it is a gift from the higher realms? The Higher Self might actually be guiding the dowsing tool's actions. Alternatively, here is one possibility with which the reader might agree: We all exist in a universe filled with energy. Every living organism is surrounded by various types of energy and is also composed of energetic forces. Animals can sense positive and negative energy and so can we. Some call this type of awareness a "sixth sense," while others describe it as "intuition" and "sensory perception." Salmon rely on it to return to their birthplace in order to spawn; birds use it for migration;

and it ensures that bees go back to their hive. How many times have you known who was calling before you lifted the phone receiver or opened the front door? Perhaps when we dowse with rods or pendulums we are also activating this inner sense?

Before dowsing with a willow branch and metal rods it is important to be quite specific about what exactly you want to find. Attempting to discover "just anything" will bring no rewards. You must clearly define in your mind and/or out loud that you are looking for water, old coins, ancient bones, etc. Dowsing within an old house can sometimes reveal where spirit activity is most prevalent. I have done this with metal rods in my home, which was built in 1894, and I found the source of the frequent 'activity' that we have witnessed since moving in eight years ago. There is a column of energy, roughly 3 ft in diameter, which runs straight down through the house. It appears to be a portal, or gateway, through which spirits come and go.

In this chapter I am focusing on pendulums that incorporate crystals, therefore, if you want to incorporate the help of the mineral kingdom when dowsing with metal rods, keep in mind that there is probably some type of ore within their metal compound. Ideally rods of copper or silver could be excellent dowsing tools, but you would need to have some method of angling one end of each rod. If you prefer to use a willow branch, carry a cleansed Clear Quartz crystal in a pocket while you are walking about and dowsing. Before you begin, ask the crystal to work in conjunction with the wooden rod so that you can easily pinpoint whatever you are seeking. As always, remember to cleanse and thank the crystal when you have finished dowsing.

Being specific about what you want to find is also necessary if you are dowsing with a pendulum. I have dowsed for ley lines on several occasions, both indoors and outside, with a Smoky Quartz pendulum. When I locate a line, the pendulum's point seems to be pulled slightly off at an angle almost as though being attracted by a magnet. It then follows the direction of the ley line. Before beginning such an exercise I take a few minutes to concentrate on my goal and express the thought that I do not want to be shown anything other than ley lines.

If a pendulum is being consulted for "Yes" and "No" answers, you will need to establish, before you begin to dowse, how your pendulum will show you these answers. For some people a pendulum will swing clockwise for "Yes" and anti-clockwise for "No." For others it will show the affirmative by swinging up-and-down, and from side-to-side for a negative response. Take time before attempting any dowsing exercises to become familiar with how your pendulum indicates its answers to you. If you already have a pendulum that is made from a mineral, I would recommend that you use it for dowsing because your endeavors will be focused and enhanced by crystalline power. However, if that is not possible, there are several other options for incorporating minerals into your endeavors. These can be pursued quite easily and I list one of them in the exercise below:

*   *   *

A Dowsing Exercise with a Ring Pendulum

- Decide upon a number of questions that you or someone else would like to have answered.
- Choose a cleansed {select an appropriate method from Appendix Four} silver or gold ring. Even if it has no gemstones, it was created from a mineral.
- Tie a piece of thread to the ring. It should be no more than 7" long.
- Sit down comfortably and practice holding your ring pendulum in your dominant hand. The official position is known as "the eye of the cobra," which means holding your forearm in an upright position and slightly away from the body. The end of the thread is held between the thumb and first finger with the other fingers following the curve of that finger. The pendulum should be hanging straight down and parallel to your arm.
- Take time to establish how this pendulum will indicate "Yes" and "No" answers.
- When you feel ready, give the pendulum a slight swing.
- Now ask your first question and wait for an answer.
- Once it is given, hold the ring still for a moment, and then give the pendulum a slight swing once again.
- Ask the next question and wait for an answer.
- Continue in this manner until all of the questions have been asked and answered.
- Thank the ring and cleanse it by visualization.

N. B. If the ring pendulum should become still when you ask a question and does not indicate a "Yes" or "No" answer, then you are being told that it is not right to be given an answer at this time. If it appears undecided, in other words, it keeps alternating between clockwise and anti-clockwise, or between up-and-down and from side-to-side, then consider this to be a "Maybe" answer.

Epilogue

If I was to be asked what my years of experience with the mineral kingdom have taught me, it is this—there is far more I do not yet understand about crystals and gemstones than what I do know. Some people consider me to have many insights into their amazing attributes, but I recognize that I am a novice when confronted with their profound possibilities. Much of the knowledge I have been given about minerals has come primarily from them and I continue to learn more about these beautiful friends. Like us, the mineral kingdom came directly from the Divine, and it exists with us in order for us to achieve healing, as well as to explore our spirituality. It is specifically the Healer of Grief, the devastating pain we experience due to the spiritual, mental, emotional and physical burdens we carry with us throughout our many incarnations. Our separation from Oneness is our eternal sorrow, but the mineral kingdom reminds us that we are never alone and that we will ultimately reunite with the Divine.

The previous chapters will have given the reader some basic understanding about how crystals can be incorporated into several different metaphysical endeavors. However, the full spectrum has certainly not been displayed here. Crystals can be brought into sessions of Aromatherapy, Reflexology, Shiatsu, Massage, Homeopathy, Acupuncture, etc. If the reader is practicing Tai Chi or Qigong, s/he should find it helpful to add crystals to the exercises in a similar manner as given in the chapter about Yoga. The reader may also be exploring divination in ways other than those put forward in this book and s/he would enhance such practices with the help of crystalline power. It is even possible to use tumblestones as divination tools. An example is given in Appendix Eight.

Young children often collect pebbles and stones, which are types of minerals. Perhaps when we are small we have an inner awareness of our spiritual connection to the mineral kingdom. As we move into adulthood, many of us forget this relationship and we disregard all but the gemstones that are fashioned into pieces of jewelry. It is possible this inner memory loss is partly due to being taught that many things, such as rocks, are inanimate. They are not alive, as we are, and this belief places a much lower value on them. We are encouraged to consider only that which is animate as being worthy of our interest.

With this mindset firmly in place it is not surprising that logic tells us a mineral specimen cannot change in any way unless we do something physically to it, e.g. carve, polish, or tumble it. However, when working with the mineral kingdom, the proof is soon shown that crystals, whether remaining in their natural form or carved into another shape, are capable of changing in many different ways. They can become much clearer, they can develop rainbows, veils and facets that were not evident before and/or facets and veils can vanish completely. Their colors can intensify, lessen, or even change, and they can grow new crystals. Sometimes they move their positions and even disappear from physical view and reappear in another location. I believe, when this happens, they move into the Etheric Level, and some never return. Certain ones, such as Record Keepers, can develop triangles on their surface as though an invisible hand etched them there. Anything is possible with minerals.

When I was in training at the International College of Crystal Healing, I was taught that a cloudy crystal often meant it was containing negativity. By cloudy I mean misty, I am not referring to those that are filled with veils and facets, or the growing end of a crystal that is normally cloudy. In addition, certain grades of minerals are naturally more opaque than others. These examples should not be viewed as indicative of negativity. However, cloudiness that clears quickly is often as a result of a mineral, which is filled with negativity, coming into contact with someone who respects and admires the mineral kingdom. The person cleanses the crystal by touch and without any conscious effort.

If a crystal or crystal skull is clear, but then becomes cloudy, give some thought to what it may have witnessed. The following are questions that might prove to be helpful: Has a very negative thinking/feeling/speaking person been handling the mineral specimen? Did that individual spend some time in close proximity to it, even though s/he did not actually touch it? Has there been inappropriate dissension between people in a room that houses a crystal or crystal skull? Or perhaps a person, who was sick, stayed in that same room? Is someone trying to use the crystal or crystal skull with less-than-positive intent? Obviously, if the answer is "Yes" to any of these questions, then a cleansing will be needed and the cloudiness should disappear.

I have read and heard about people using minerals as a 'catch basin' for negative energy. The negativity that is removed from someone or something is directed toward a specific crystal, and it is asked to contain this energy. Afterwards, a cleansing of the crystal takes place. In my opinion, this is not an appropriate use of a mineral, even though I am certain crystals are willing to perform this act for us. For example, Amethyst being known to freely absorb negativity. However, deliberately sending negative energy to your crystalline friend does not seem to be either loving or respectful. Asking the Divine to transmute or the Earth Mother to recycle negativity into its higher form is a much kinder procedure and will prove less stressful to the crystal.

In conclusion, I do not think any one person has yet unlocked the greater secrets of the mineral kingdom. This book reflects my own and other people's explorations into previously unchartered territory, but they are only a beginning. We are all just attempting to scratch the surface of what crystalline power can achieve. I believe the in-depth knowledge of crystals is being withheld from us because we have misused their properties in the distant past. We are not yet sufficiently evolved to steer clear of making the same mistakes again; therefore, we cannot be entrusted with such absolute power. Even so, I offer these pages with the belief that we are all becoming more compassionate and less egocentric. I sincerely hope this book will aid each reader in the exploration of her/his inner wisdom and soul's expectancy. We are spiritual beings for whom the mineral kingdom is an ally within the quest to understand ourselves through physical existence.

Crystal Blessings,
{Waxing Moon in Gemini}

Appendix One

The Crystal Skull/Tarot Card Readings

The first reading documented here is that of the woman who originated this exercise.

Jeanne Dunn's Reading with Spirit Warrior, a Red Jasper skull:

"I began this reading by lighting my favorite incense {Hummingbird} and settling in for prayers and meditation with Spirit Warrior in hand. A sense of calm settled over the room immediately, and it wasn't long before I began working with the cards. I settled Spirit Warrior on the carved box in which I keep my cards. A few shuffling passes and a three-pile cut, and we were ready to go. The cards fell as follows:

1. Me: 6 of Swords
2. Spirit Warrior: 4 of Coins
3. Challenges: 2 of Coins, reversed
4. Lessons/Growth: Knight of Coins
5. Healing/Evolution: 8 of Swords

Interpretation:

- I am in a stronger position all around now than I have been in a long time. I am moving toward successful conclusions with the aid of my crystal skull family. Spirit Warrior reminds me that the selfless attitude will prevail—a lesson that came hard in my life during my first marriage, and has endured. I am ready now for inventive, original thinking, and Spirit Warrior has been activated and will be helping me move forward in this regard. "A light has been switched on!" Life is finally becoming more orderly after years of emotional chaos, and though there are obligations still to be met, I am able to cope and have achieved a certain peace of mind.

- Spirit Warrior is a skull who will be beneficial in helping me balance energies. He is all about unity, security. Working with Spirit Warrior {or, as he shared with me, "Spiro, will do!"} may actually enable me to achieve in the material world things I feel I have attained spiritually—earthly power through wealth. The 4 of Coins indicates financial gains, usually in the form of legacies or gifts, but as the card representing Spiro, my interpretation is that I am ready to receive the gifts the skulls—Spirit Warrior and others—are so generously bestowing. The 4 of Coins can also symbolize feeling/being isolated, yet feeling secure, which is very much how I feel in my day-to-day life here in Danville, as far as my spirituality and my work with the skulls goes.

- My Challenges are highlighted by the 2 of Coins reversed. Weaknesses and strengths revolving like the two spinning coins. This is a time for me to be questioning my intents, my purposes in my spiritual work and in the material {fiscal} world. This card is all about inconsistent effort and lack of willpower. I lose focus and am too easily distracted. And I definitely need to resolve financial issues and resolve to stick to a budget. These types of obstacles definitely inhibit spiritual growth and connection with Spirit Warrior and my other skulls for the tasks at hand.

- The Knight of Coins in the position of Lessons/Growth indicates that Spirit Warrior is in my life to provoke deep thought and to encourage me to be more decided about the direction I want to take in life. This card is tied into Earth Energies, which I have always felt have been particularly strong in Red Jasper, too. The good Knight represents that a spiritual mission is about to begin. Now is the time to direct energy into being more meditative and levelheaded, which will be the real key to success. The things I need to avoid are stupidity and denying feelings of resentment or anger. Denying these things only prevents me from dealing with them, and then they fester. Spirit Warrior is here to provide discreet assistance and definitely wants to be carried about more often, so he can do me the most good. The Knight of Coins is usually representative of a capable manager who works behind the scenes, and this is a role Spirit Warrior wants me to know he is ready to handle! So it looks like I've got to make him a traveling pouch to slip into my purse!

- Healing/Evolution is shown here as the 8 of Swords. Swords are probably my least favorite suit, although one of my favorite Swords {the 6} showed up at the beginning of the reading. Swords can often be 'tough' cards, but they also 'cut through' the doo-doo and bring one straight to the point. This 8 reveals that I am currently suffering a locking-in of energies, and that this puts me in a very restrictive position in life. I feel trapped and unable to move much of the time. I lose myself in over-attention to details, in an effort to avoid the difficulties painted in the overall picture. Fear keeps me from expressing myself. This card is actually a symbol of the mind being a prison of ideas, which one cannot readily express. It causes me to feel too intense at times or to feel completely repressed. What Spirit Warrior is here to do is to show me that I cannot be repressed UNLESS I ALLOW MYSELF TO BE REPRESSED! Liberation is a choice! But it doesn't come without a price. Spirit Warrior will become the ally with whom I ponder the choices and the prices, and he will enable me to make good decisions along the path to free expression, growth and my own spiritual and personal evolution.

End Notes:

Following my work with the Tarot and jotting notes, I found myself still writing. These words came through:

- Spirit Warrior glows more brilliantly red. His eyes come alive over those expressive markings. SPIRIT Warrior—he grins—or SPIRO will do.
- I (Jeanne) cannot do spiritual work until I am firmly centered and balanced in the physical world. It is the anchor that will allow me to ride the storms, the great angry waves—and to finally rest in bliss upon the calm seas of Spirit.

- Balance—it cannot be all one way or another. One cannot shirk earthly responsibilities and hold up Spirituality as a shield. We have chosen existence in the physical world, and as such, the lives we live here are a foundation for the progress of our Souls toward the ultimate reunion with the Creator.
- Live each moment with that ecstatic goal in mind, and it will be as natural as breathing to approach Life from a position of Patience, Kindness and Love. It becomes easier to live a life of Truth. One's OWN Truth—for what other Truth is there?
- The spark of divinity dwells in each person. The skulls are our allies in the pursuit of nurturing that spark until it bursts into flame, and our Light expands to touch the lives of those around us.
- This is the Message that comes through Spirit Warrior this evening."

*　　*　　*

Linda Cody's Reading with Polaris, a Whale Bone Fossil skull:

"I selected my lovely whale bone fossil skull, Polaris, who is very quiet and mysterious with me, although he sent a beautiful vision to Michele of a whale leaping out of the water in the night time. I also selected Huerfano {my new jawless Clear Quartz skull}, who seems very intriguing to me. I lit a candle, set Polaris and Huerfano sitting on their decks—Polaris on a Robin Wood Tarot, and Huerfano on a Power Deck by Lynn C. Andrews, which is not a Tarot deck at all—and subjected the poor things to a few minutes of my wretched recorder playing. {My pug dog howled in accompaniment.}

I then meditated with Polaris, who has a "1,000-yard stare." He always seems to be staring out at nothing, but by the end of the meditation, I felt he was 'looking' at me, and I felt more connected. I shuffled and dealt the deck, as directed, and this is what I got:

1. Me: Ace of Pentacles
2. Polaris: 5 of Swords
3. Challenges: Page of Swords
4. Lessons/Growth: 1—The Magician
5. Healing/Evolution: 18—The Moon

Interpretation:

- Me: Ace of Pentacles—My current state of mind and circumstances, and how this affects my perception of interaction with Polaris. Pure contentment, attainment, prosperity, bright prospects, both material and spiritual. {Well, this must refer to the spiritual, since my material prospects are pretty horrible at the moment!}
- Polaris: 5 of Swords—What is required to establish rapport? What does Polaris need from me? Failure, defeat, degradation, trickery, cowardice, manipulation. {Please tell me a positive way to look at this!}
- Challenges: Page of Swords—What is holding me back in life and/or preventing me from connecting with Polaris? Vigilance, agility, insight, keenness of vision. {Huh?}
- Lessons/Growth: The Magician—My ability/willingness to learn from Polaris. {This, at least, seems pretty positive.} Opportunities to use talents, creativity, originality, skill, diplomacy, self-reliance, merging of the Four Elements.
- Healing/Evolution: The Moon—What aspects of myself/life will Polaris help me heal? A warning, deception, enemies who are out of sight—a caution to stay on your path for safety. Darkness, companions who are out of their element.

The best way I found to look at all of this is: I am at a stage in my life where I am ripe for spiritual growth {Ace of Pentacles}. Polaris needs for me to give up my sense of failure, my feeling that I have wasted my life and that it is too late to find my true calling {5 of Swords}. Maybe I'm a little too practical, and not enough of a dreamer {Page of Swords}. Polaris can help me explore my talents and skills in new ways, and develop parts of myself that I've deemed too "impractical" {The Magician}. In doing this, I will begin healing from the damage that others have done to me {The Moon}. In becoming more self-reliant, the opinions of others will matter less, and I can finally rise above the useless, painful cycle of comparing myself to others, and always finding myself lacking."

* * *

Linda Cody's Reading with Huerfano, a Clear Quartz skull:

"Huerfano's spread was different; being a non-Tarot deck. I have paraphrased and taken bits of what the cards said.

1. Me: Innocence—To live in civilization, we conform to fit in with the crowd. But to maintain your receptive innocence, you must listen to your inner voice.
2. Huerfano: Feminine—Woman is the Keeper of the Mother Earth, but the world is ordered according to male consciousness—even language is a barrier between Mother Earth and her children. Feminine consciousness is needed for world harmony.
3. Challenges: Aspiration—Aspiration is your aim spiritually and physically in the world and involves the totality of your being. Without the balance between the physical and the spiritual, aspiration is a hollow accomplishment.
4. Lessons/Growth: Nurturing—We are the only ones who can heal ourselves—sometimes with assistance, sometimes without. The earth's energy corresponds with our energy/chakra system, and we heal each other. Prayer enables you to take power out of the mind and place it in the hands of the deities of the earth and sky. Nurture your dreams and your spirit.
5. Healing/Evolution: Individuality—Seeking approval is based on self-doubt. Power lies in individuality and in the ability to see yourself through your own eyes and not through the eyes of another.

Interpretation:

My best interpretation here is:

- I am ready to listen to my intuition, which has led me to the skulls and to Huerfano specifically.
- Huerfano needs me to tune into my intuition and feelings, not words and language, when I am communing with him.
- I need to find a better balance between the physical and spiritual in my life, instead of separating the two.
- I see the skulls as an opportunity to find healing for myself, and hope to work with them to that end.

- And, like the Tarot reading, the main message seems to be to follow the path for my own sake, and not worry so much about how I appear to others."

* * *

Elaine Simmons's Reading with Andromeda, a Brazilian Clear Quartz skull:

"This reading was done with Andromeda, a Brazilian crystal skull. I used the Goddess Tarot deck. I smudged with sage/cedar/sweet grass, had a small purple candle burning, and played a CD of various choirs singing different types of spiritual music.

1. Me: 6 of Pentacles
2. Andromeda: 13—Transformation {Death}
3. Challenges: 10 of Pentacles
4. Lessons/Growth: 7 of Cups
5. Healing/Evolution: 5 of Pentacles
6. Extra Card: 3 of Wands, reversed

Interpretation:

- Me: 6 of Pentacles—I am "sharing talents" with others; in this case my mother is taking lots of my time, especially the last few months. I'm also continuing to see clients, although on a limited basis, for counseling and hypnotherapy. The skulls may be among those 'begging' for attention. {I'm basing this in large part on the particular illustration for this card in this deck.}
- The Skull: Death—What an appropriate card for a skull! Perhaps Andromeda would like to teach me that I need to clear a space in my life to make room for the new. The need to allow something to die. To create life out of death.
- Challenges: 10 of Pentacles—This is generally a really nice card. Here I would say that it is going to be a challenge for me to create this "home and family" with this skull, or perhaps the skulls as a whole, in the way I would like.
- Lessons/Growth: 7 of Cups—I am being distracted by all my many and varied interests, as well as by my responsibilities. It illustrates very

well how bombarded I've been feeling about even what I most need to do in the next few minutes, weeks, years. And I came back from California with a puppy this last time, just what I needed! My older dog really likes the company, and that's the main reason I did it, but still it further divides my attention.

- Healing/Evolution: 5 of Pentacles—Now, this is not one of my favorite cards, of course. What I think it means here is that I'm going to be forced to look within for greater resources, or at least to focus better on what I really want to create with this skull; and that I will need to confront my fears in order for the healing/evolution to take place, or I may not be able to accomplish it.

I took one more card to see if it could shed more light on #5. It was the 3 of Wands, reversed. There may be a delay in achieving success, or perhaps it isn't even realistic that it will happen at this time.

So there is the quick version. I've done the reading with one other skull since then—the lovely Shiva Lingham, Temple."

I asked Elaine if she thought having the skull present during the reading was helpful or a hindrance to understanding what the cards were displaying. She answered:

"I'm not absolutely sure that Andromeda's presence helped with interpreting the cards, but I think that it did. I pick up other people's thoughts frequently, sometimes without knowing it, and I know it happens with the skulls, too, and having her there was certainly a focus for the reading. I'm not sure I could/would want to do it without the skull right there as the central focus."

*   *   *

Deb Chenneour Williams's Reading with a Rose Quartz skull:

"I finally had a chance to do the Bridge Reading and below is what I got. I haven't read cards for a long time so I'm a little rusty. If anybody sees anything that I didn't, please feel free to jump in.

I chose a small Rose Quartz, stylized skull that was supposed to have belonged to Melody {*Love is in the Earth* series author}. I originally got this skull just because it was Melody's, a kind of collector's item. It has given me no name and basically it just is there/here. This is the only skull that I have here that has not revealed anything to me and it was also the only one that would allow itself to speak through the Tarot cards. I used the small card version of the Rider Waite deck.

I did my usual pre-reading quiet time, with Indra Sandal incense, calling on the Highest Forces of Light and asking for guidance and protection. This is automatic with me, so it's a bit hard to detail what I do. I then shuffled in the question: "How will I establish communication or a connection with this crystal skull?" As a result of this, I heard this voice tell me that a connection was not needed and that this particular skull would communicate with me in an 'as needed' mode. So I proceeded to re-shuffle in the question "Do you currently have a message for me?" I had much better results with that question.

1. Me: 19—The Sun
2. The Skull: 2 of Cups, reversed
3. Challenges: 13—Death, reversed
4. Lessons/Growth: 20—Judgment, reversed
5. Healing/Evolution: 12—The Hanged Man, reversed

Interpretation:

- Me: The Sun—I'm tired and frustrated. I'm totally upset because the future is so uncertain. I MUST remember—one step at a time. Right actions today means the sun will shine tomorrow.
- The Skull: 2 of Cups, reversed—I need to let it be known what is needed and let it go, put it in the 'hands' of the Higher Forces.
- Challenges: Death, reversed—Many changes are to come and a negative situation will end. Phoenix /me rising!!!
- Lessons/Growth: Judgment, reversed—I must learn to accept gifts {physical, mental and spiritual} as they will be for my own highest good and will assist the Phoenix to rise.
- Healing/Evolution: The Hanged Man, reversed—Let go and let the Higher Forces act!!! The problems will be resolved one by one. The Phoenix will rise!!!

After I had finished with this layout, I heard a voice tell me that was the message, to pay attention and to allow me to rest. I don't know if this little Rose Quartz was supposed to stay with Melody or if it was worked too hard before, but it just seems to want to sit in the basket with a bunch of the rock kids. It seems very content there. It did also mention that I would do better to work with true friends, meaning the other skulls. I did ask if it was supposed to find another home. It said, "No" and that it was safe here."

*　　*　　*

Douglas Ratcliff's Reading with Electric Blue, a Pietersite skull:

"After finding two Major Arcana cards missing from my Rider Waite Tarot deck I decided to give the Enochian deck another try. I've had this deck for over ten years, but haven't really looked at it since reading the book that came with it, partly because at the time I wasn't empathetic to the symbolism of the deck. The Enochian deck is different from standard Tarot decks in that the standard Tarot is based on the Kabbalistic Tree of Life, whereas the Enochian Tarot is based on the Enochian Magic system first set down by Sir John Dee of the court of Elizabeth I. There are 30 cards in the Enochian Major Arcana, representing Aethyrs and 56 cards of the Minor Arcana, representing deities or entities that inhabit regions of the four Great Watchtowers, the suits being Fire, which corresponds to Wands, Water, which corresponds to Cups, Air, which corresponds to Swords, and Earth, which corresponds to Pentacles.

The way I did the reading was right after laying out the cards. I looked at the whole and my impression was that this was a somewhat ominous reading, but, ultimately, I see it as positive that Electric Blue is here to lead me through a series of changes that will allow me mastery of myself in a way I can't even begin to understand right now. Well, that's what I think now; my first impression was it was ominous, but ultimately positive. After glimpsing the 'big picture,' I wrote down my impression of each card, about a page per card, since it has been so long since I worked with this deck.

Then I took the five cards and studied them before bed and asked for help in understanding this reading. I only remember bits and pieces of dreams, last night's being the best, but I still only tangentially understand. I will be referring to The Enochian Tarot by Gerald and Betty Schueler and my own notes.

1. Me: Archangels of Water
2. The Skull: The Higher Self
3. Challenges: The Babe
4. Lessons/Growth: Babalon
5. Healing/Evolution: The Abyss

Interpretation:

- Me: Archangels of Water—This card can almost be said to represent change for change's sake. It depicts the sixteen Archangels of Water creating a whirlpool. They could be said to be the personification of Time because their mission is to make sure things change and remain in motion. I see this card in this reading as representing a doorway. I am the doorway and I bring change to whoever enters my life, whether I want to or not. This is just my function. But I've always had trouble bringing change for me, or at least the changes I feel I need to make, and so I called out and this Pietersite skull I nicknamed "Electric Blue" answered.

- The Skull: The Higher Self—I immediately felt this was an answer from my Higher Self, who I constantly talk to, and that Electric Blue is a direct manifestation. The card depicts a very old man. I felt he was very wise and complete. He holds a cup and staff at arm's length from each other, which I took to mean discipline over sensuality. In the background, the Enochian goddess, Babalon, rides a domesticated beast reinforcing this theme. The King in the foreground represents the past, his kingdom is already gone and he is waiting to die. Babalon is bringing the future. Electric Blue is here to change the very order of my life. The old order is passed. The Archangels of Water and the Higher Self are in agreement. Specifically, the Higher Self represents a change for the better and the Archangels of Water represent changes that must be obeyed lest a heavy karmic penalty be paid. I desire change and all signs indicate change is coming and it will be for the best. So then what are the challenges to achieving this change?

- Challenges: The Babe—Originally, I felt this indicated a need to look at things with new eyes, but now I feel the Babe is telling me that comfort or complacency in my current lifestyle is the biggest challenge. The Babe is the first card of the Major Arcana in the Enochian system, the Babe in Blue represents the "auric egg and the monadic essence of man," which is to say we are monadic beings that split our experience into the "I" and the "not-I." Above the Babe is a barrier to the higher spiritual realms, further reinforcing the idea of a challenge.

- Lessons/Growth: Babalon {Ba ba loh en}—Babalon is the chief goddess of the Enochian systems. An interesting note is that her name means "the attraction of sound," which the Schuelers inform us is identical to the tantric Shabda. The reason I find this note worthy is it reminds me of the Skull Song. This card is associated with intense bliss, intense joy and worldly happiness. The meaning of this card in this place in the reading seems so obvious to me that I'm probably missing it, but I feel that Babalon is telling me to partake in some worldly pleasure and to enjoy myself, and so this is what Electric Blue is here to teach me—not to take things so seriously. If I could learn this, I think it would be a major accomplishment.

- Healing/Evolution: The Abyss—This is perhaps the most ominous card; it depicts the arch demon Khoronzon, who guards the gulf between our world of form and the higher worlds of formlessness. My first impression, when seeing this card, was self-mastery. Putting it into the context of the reading, I think I am being told, if I can overcome the barrier of complacency and learn to let go and enjoy life a little, I'll be much more balanced. I'll have both work and play, for example.

So to recap, I desire change; I am the embodiment of change. Electric Blue is here to bring me change, if I can overcome my complacency and learn to let go and enjoy myself and cultivate some desires. I won't lose anything, but will gain the ability to move between the world of pleasure and the world of work—mastery of myself and the world."

*   *   *

Andrea Wright's Reading with Yorik, a Rutilated Quartz skull:

"After meditating and preparing for the spread, I picked up the deck to shuffle. I saw the bottom card, GLARING at me, and it was the Devil. I shuddered, but took it in. He was there for a reason. This deck is the Intuitive Tarot so I was to go on my gut instincts.

1. Me: The Devil
2. The Skull: 6 Of Rods
3. Challenges: 4 of Swords
4. Lessons/Growth: 5 of Swords
5. Healing/Evolution: 6 of Swords

Interpretation:

- Me: The Devil—My heart literally skipped a beat when I saw this. I was so shocked I had to read up on him. The figure is androgynous and he has no mouth, he seems impatient to communicate {which is very much me right now}. By his feet are two naked people {male and a female}, standing in the flames. They are not chained or bound there, they can move of their own free will, but haven't. To me, this means that I have my own weaknesses, demons and fears to deal with. I thought I knew them all and was coping OK. But this card apparently is trying to tell me that there are some deeper hidden fears that need my attention. I think Yorik will be bringing to the fore some issues that have been kept under lock and key and forgotten about. I have to set this free, or turn and use it for my progression instead of my own destruction.

- Yorik: 6 of Rods—This card seems to be the pole opposite of me. Here I am being shown that Yorik has had to struggle and take a long journey to achieve his enlightenment. The card shows a triumphant figure, standing elevated and at the end of a road, arms outstretched and facing the white disc of the sunset. I think he is inviting me here, showing me it is possible. The journey will be a long one, but it is achievable. He is encouraging me.

- Challenges: 4 of Swords—Here the image is of a peaceful man, sitting in meditation and contemplation. There is a beam of white light shining down on his head. Around him are the four swords, equally spaced and symbolizing protection. This makes perfect sense to me; it has been so long since I meditated regularly. I am finding it hard to get back into it, relaxing, regulating my breathing, protecting myself properly. Yet when I perform Reiki on another person, it flows so easily. I can and want to do these things for other people, yet when it comes to myself, half measures are involved. This card tells me that I need to spend more 'quiet time' with myself, searching my own depths to attain the kind of tranquility represented by the figure on the card. The four swords are showing me the level of protection I need whilst in this happy state. They make it steadfast and solid.

- Lessons/Growth: 5 of Swords—Although the Devil had the strongest impact on me due to the sheer horror of it, this card is the one that stays in the fore front of my mind. It has a couple of meanings for me. At the front of the card a woman lies naked and vulnerable in the fetal position. She is at the foot of an imposing figure. He holds his sword upright with one hand, showing he is not threatening, but is strong and willful. The card shows me the two sides of my personality, the dark, imposing, dominating and bossy side of me, but really, I am vulnerable with the need for affection and nurturing a child would receive. The other way it shows itself to me is that a 'Master' or 'Teacher' has stripped me down, humiliating me and almost scolding me, as if to say, "I can see right through you. Now you are naked, how will you build yourself?" This is a very hard lesson for me to learn. Sometimes humiliation can be your best teacher when you learn to accept the truth. This has happened to me several times on my travels, meeting people and they tell me what they see. The lesson hurts, but you can always be better for it when you deal with the ugliness. This may be telling me to "Stop being weak {among so many other things}. Stand up and get on with it. Be humble and accept the lessons coming your way." I have always been used to teaching people spirituality, Crystal Healing and Reiki. These are not everyday things, so when I meet someone who is interested, but not familiar, I teach them what I know. I have joined two groups and I am at the bottom of the 'pecking' order. I am now the pupil and I must listen with an open heart.

- Healing/Evolution: 6 of Swords—This was a nice card to see at the end of the reading. At last, something truly positive in every sense. The image is of a boat with three people in it, a seemingly old fellow steering the boat for a parental figure and his/her child. They are naked, but for a white sheet, which is falling down. It is their journey. At the end of the river are the six swords, symbolizing and 'opening' into something. The journey is at an end, and they have made it through the hardest part. It is all "easy sailing from here on in," as the saying goes. The water is calm and blue. I'm glad this card came because the previous four showed me that hard times are ahead, but it will all be worth it. I can do this, but as the old fellow pushing the boat represents, I don't have to do it alone.

I've not used any form of Tarot for so long. Yet with the help of this particular spread and Yorik, the message seemed very clear and appropriate to my life right now. I have to stand tall and take the punches, I think. I like to think that I am a strong person. Aided by stubbornness, I refuse to be intimated or have another person impose their will and fear on me. Maybe that is how well I connected with these cards; I have only had them for two days, and haven't had another downfall. Refusing the fear maybe hindering my ability to see the lesson it brings."

Appendix Two

The Mohs Scale of Hardness for Minerals[1]

Frederick Mohs {1773-1839} was a German mineralogist who defined the hardness of minerals by means of a scale from 1 {softest} to 10 {hardest}. This is an example of his scale:

1—Talc
2—Gypsum—e.g. Selenite, Alabaster
3—Calcite
3.5—Azurite
4—Fluorite
4.5—Apophyllite
5—Apatite
5.5—Lazurite
6—Orthoclase Feldspar—e.g. Moonstone, Amazonite
6.5—Opal
7—Quartz—e.g. Aventurine, Tigereye
7.5—Beryl—e.g. Emerald, Aquamarine
8—Topaz
9—Corundum—e.g. Sapphire, Ruby
10—Diamond

1. Marion Webb-De Sisto, *Crystal Skulls*, p. 169.

Appendix Three

Negative Energy within Minerals[1]

The following are some of the more common causes of crystals becoming 'dirty' by holding onto negativity:

- Mining, particularly by means of blasting—this is considered extremely traumatic for minerals.
- Minerals that grew near or on a negative ley line—there has been some speculation on the affects of negative ley lines on humans, but not on minerals.
- Negative events having happened on the surface above where the minerals grew—e.g. battles, massacres, etc. or any evil act played out within a location some distance above the 'home' of minerals. The negative energy from the event would not only cling to the ground surface, but would also seep far down into the planet, pass through the minerals located there and some of it would become trapped within them.
- Bartering—whether between the mine owner and the wholesaler, the wholesaler and the retailer, or the retailer and the customer, this can create negative energy. The minerals in question would be close by and possibly even in view of the individuals bartering and, where there is disagreement over money, there is negativity.
- Intentional misuse—there are individuals who, understanding the power of the mineral kingdom, deliberately tap into that force by using a mineral specimen to enhance, magnify and focus their evil thoughts and actions.

- Unintentional misuse—some people may not realize the potential that lies within minerals. If any are nearby when they are thinking or acting upon their negative intentions toward others, then those minerals will pick up some of that negativity.
- Healing and therapeutic situations—clients release physical, emotional, mental and spiritual pain when they receive healing, and this is a form of negativity. If any type of mineral, whether in its original form or reshaped by carving, is being used as part of the healing or therapeutic modality, it will absorb some of that adverse energy.

In the following examples, if a crystal or any mineral is in the same physical area as the occurrences given, the resulting effect on the specimen will be detrimental:

- Long-term illness and death—when someone is long-term sick or dying, there is pain and unhappiness associated with this event and this can be seen as negativity.
- Unhappy or negatively thinking/feeling people—a person who is sad, depressed, or of a pessimistic disposition, creates negative energy.
- Unhappy, stressful, upsetting, frightening, arguing, and/or violent situations—any of these events will cause a negative atmosphere.
- Unpleasant paranormal occurrences—if a building, a room, or any area is subject to hauntings and spirit attachments that are not of a positive nature, then negativity is present.
- Dirty surroundings—when a place is not physically clean, this generates negative energy.

Finally and as previously documented, it is known that the mineral Amethyst, which is a member of the Quartz Family, has a natural tendency to attract and store negative energy within itself. Therefore, all Amethyst crystals, geodes, clusters, together with any carvings from this mineral, will need cleansing on a regular basis.

1. Marion Webb-De Sisto, *Crystal Skulls*, pp. 126-128.

Appendix Four

Cleansing Crystals[1]

Before using any of the methods below, affirm that the negativity, which you are removing from any crystal, is transmuted to the Divine so that it may reach its highest, positive form.

Using Sound:

- Tibetan singing bowls, bells, cymbals, or tuning forks—hold a few inches above the crystal and make sound by hitting, striking, etc. several times.
- Chanting, singing, or reciting poems—hold the crystal while doing these.
- Place on a piano or an electric organ—be careful that the vibration, when the instrument is being played, does not dislodge the crystal and cause it to fall.
- Play tapes/CDs of classical music, New Age music, or sounds of nature, e.g. birdsong, waterfalls, whale songs, etc.—place the crystal in the proximity of the music or sounds.

Using Other Crystals:*

- Place on an Amethyst bed—in order to avoid scratches and damage to the crystal, place and remove it carefully and gently, especially if it is made from a softer mineral than Quartz. Once the crystal is removed, immediately cleanse the Amethyst bed because it will have absorbed some of the negativity.

- Place in a circle of cleansed crystals—use those that are of a similar size to the one being cleansed. The crystal circle is not absorbing the negativity; it is helping to direct it to the Divine.
- Place in a circle of cleansed crystal skulls—position the surrounding skulls facing in toward the crystal to be cleansed. The skull circle is not absorbing the negativity; it is helping to direct it to the Divine.

* These methods should not be used if the crystal is very 'dirty' or has been greatly misused because it may deeply infect the other crystals, bed, or skulls. All crystal and skull circles used in the above methods should be cleansed immediately afterwards in the event some trace of negative energy may have been absorbed.

Using Nature, the Earth Mother and the Plant Kingdom:

- Place in a bed of dried flower petals—this works particularly well with rose petals.
- Place in a bed of sage leaves, cedar chips, or sweet grass—if none of these are readily available, but you have smudge sticks, break one apart and use its contents because these are usually made from sage and/or sweet grass.
- Bury in the garden—place a marker in the event you forget where the crystal is buried.
- Bury in a pot of soil, peat, or sand—again, place a marker so that the pot is not used for a plant.
- Place in full moonlight—even if the moon is hidden behind the clouds, the full moon energy will have a positive effect on the crystal.
- Place in bright sunlight**—a windowsill facing East will bring the healing rays of the morning sun, as well as heat that is less intense.
- Hang in a net in a tree or bush, allowing the breeze to cleanse it—ensure that the net is secure in order to avoid it becoming loose and the crystal falling out.
- Place within an ancient stone circle or close to a standing stone—spending time in these sacred places will be beneficial for you, too.
- Wrap in silk or another natural fiber—you could also make a bag out of the material, and place the crystal in it when you take it anywhere with you.

- Stroke with a feather—traditionally this should be an eagle feather, but it is very unlikely that you will have one of these, therefore, any feather that you find, while outdoors, will work well.

** Not suitable for Amethyst, Fluorite and Smoky Quartz as the sun will fade the colors of these minerals.

The following methods are only for crystals and minerals with a hardness number of 7* or above:

- Leave outside in the rain—only suitable if you are sure that it is not acid rain that is falling.
- Place in the sea, a lake, a river, or a stream—keep a close eye on the crystal, if it is quite small, because the movement of water, particularly that of the tide, can take it out beyond your reach.
- Place in a solution of spring water and 2 drops of the Bach Flower Remedy Crab Apple—the essence of the crab apple tree is very cleansing.
- In addition, add 4 drops of Bach Rescue Remedy—if you believe the crystal has been traumatized in some way.
- Place in a solution of spring water and essential oil(s), e.g. Juniper, Rosemary, Lemon—these are considered cleansing, but if you have other essential oil preferences, use those instead.
- Hold under running water or place in sea salt water—hold the crystal firmly, while it is under the running water, so that it does not slip out of your hand.

* See Appendix Two.

Using Other Methods:

- Trace sacred symbols on the crystal's surface or place it in/on a sacred geometric pattern—symbols can be traced with your finger directly onto the crystal. Draw the geometric shape on paper with pen or pencil.
- Give healing to the crystal, e.g. Reiki, but if you are not a 'hands-on' healer, hold the crystal and mentally send it loving thoughts.
- Place inside a pyramid—the metal frame type of pyramid, but if by any chance you are visiting the pyramids in Egypt or Mexico, then most definitely take the crystal with you.

- Rotate a pendulum clockwise over the crystal—particularly effective if the pendulum is also made from a crystal.
- Give loving gestures to the crystal—e.g. kisses, cuddles, or gentle strokes.
- Pass through the smoke of burning incense or smudge sticks—I have found that smudging works very well on Amethyst.
- Pass through a candle flame—be careful not to burn your fingers.
- Place on an altar, a shrine, or within a sacred space—you can designate an area within your home as a sacred space by bringing into it candles, incense, a water fountain, crystals, a Buddha, a Goddess ornament, a Menorah, a Madonna, or any spiritual effigy that is meaningful to you.
- Visualize Divine Light passing through the crystal—imagine this as being golden, or white, or a rainbow of colors.
- Visualize holding it under a Divine waterfall—if you imagine that you are also standing under the waterfall while holding the crystal, you will receive healing, as well.
- Visualize different colors passing through the crystal—blue and green are considered healing colors, but use whichever ones you feel are appropriate.

1. Marion Webb-De Sisto, *Crystal Skulls*, pp. 129-133.

Appendix Five

Dedicating and Tuning Crystals[1]

Dedication:

The concept of dedication is to ensure that, should your crystal or crystal skull fall into the hands of someone who would wish to misuse its properties, her/his attempts to do so will be thwarted. It is as though you are placing a shield of protection all around the mineral specimen. Within this procedure you are dedicating the mineral specimen to the highest realms and asking that it can only be used for the very highest good. Dedication is performed immediately after the original cleansing process, which should take place as soon as a new crystal has arrived in your home.

I learned how to dedicate a mineral specimen during my training at the International College of Crystal Healing. We were encouraged to create our own personal dedication ritual, keeping it simple and direct, and the following words are how I dedicate all of my crystals and crystal skulls. The reader is welcome to copy them exactly or add to and alter these words as needed. Having cleansed the crystal/crystal skull in some manner, I sit holding it in my hands with my eyes closed. Then I say:

> "I dedicate this crystal/crystal skull to Love, Light and the Highest Good so that the Oneness may come again. I ask that it be used with only the very Highest, Finest and Purest intentions and that only the very Highest, Finest and Purest vibrations are allowed to pass through it. So be it, so be it, and so it is."

Y ou can substitute your own words or even add a prayer for the dedication. Whatever feels comfortable and right for you will work best. You can also light a candle and/or burn incense while performing the dedication. This is particularly helpful when you are dedicating several crystals and mineral specimens at the same time.

Tuning:

Before beginning to work with your crystal or crystal skull, you will need to tune it to whatever purpose you have in mind. Whether for regression, healing, channeling, or scrying, you are asking the mineral specimen to focus on the work with which you want it to help you. Some people call this process "programming," others think of it as "activating" the crystal/crystal skull. I am comfortable with the word "tuning" and it is the one I always use. When I tune a crystal friend, I am stating the work with which I need help. I am asking for its assistance. While asking for help, I qualify this request by stating that I should only be given it if what I want is right and appropriate for me or for a client.

Crystals and crystal skulls can be tuned and retuned as frequently as required. They can also be tuned to more than one task at the same time. So ask for crystalline help and it will be given.

1.   Marion Webb-De Sisto, *Crystal Skulls*, pp. 133-135.

Appendix Six

Earthing/Grounding Crystals

All minerals of the following colors are earthing/grounding—black, brown, red and orange. The specimens used can be large, especially when it is estimated that a person will easily become ungrounded. They can be in their rough state or carved and polished into skulls, spheres, obelisks, etc. The following is a list of some earthing examples, but it is not exhaustive:

Black Obsidian {including Snowflake, Rainbow, Mahogany, Gold or Silver Sheen}
Basalt
Tourmaline {when black or brown}
Black Onyx
Ferberite
Marble {in any of the above four colors}
Spinel {when red, brown, or black}
Augite {when brown or black}
Hornblende {when brown or black}
Actinolite {when black}
Goethite {when brown or black}
Smoky Quartz
Brown/Gold Tigereye
Tigeriron
Sedonite
Honey Calcite
Garnet

Cuprite
Huebnerite {when red or orange}
Fire Opal
Cinnabar {when red or brownish red}
Ruby
Red Jasper
Red Calcite
Rubellite
Realgar {when red or orange}
Wulfenite {when orange or brown}
Scheelite {when orange or brown}
Orange Calcite
Carnelian
Sard

These other minerals and substances have also been found to possess grounding properties:

Jet
Petrified Wood
Petrified Mud
Fossils
Stromatolite
Hematite
Boji Stones
Pyrite
Sandstone
Ebony {a type of very hard wood}
Red Coral

An earthing crystal should be placed at the feet, between the thighs, or underneath a massage couch in line with the Root/Base Chakra. It is the first crystal to be placed at the commencement of a session and the last one to be removed at its end.

N. B. Do not forget to cleanse earthing crystals before and after use.

Other Earthing/Grounding Strategies:

Eating fruits and vegetables is a grounding activity, as is consuming anything which contains ingredients that originally grew as a plant, crop, etc., e.g. flour, oats, or sugar. This is possibly because all of these edibles plunged their roots into the ground as they grew and, therefore, received her earthing energies. All root vegetables and potatoes are very grounding, they actually grew beneath the ground. For some people drinking water or fruit and vegetable juices is grounding, too. Doing any earthly activity, even if it is boring work, helps keep us anchored to the earth plane. Pot holing and exploring underground caves and caverns will earth our soaring souls. Handling clay, soil, sand, etc. is grounding, therefore, potters and sculptors should be well-grounded individuals. When we do gardening, we are also grounded as we dig into the soil and plant shrubs, trees, flowers and such. Hugging trees helps to earth our 'spacey' energy as does standing barefoot in mud, soil, sand, or standing/sitting/lying on the grass.

A Further Note on Earthing/Grounding:

When I began my metaphysical pursuits some twenty-four years ago, I had no idea that I was a real 'space cadet.' Whenever I attempted meditation and after a minute or two, I would be gone somewhere. Sometime later, I would return. At first, I thought I must be falling asleep because I could recall nothing from my attempted meditations. This frustrated me because I knew a person was supposed to gain peace and a better sense of spiritual awareness from these exercises. However, I always felt relaxed when I returned to conscious awareness, even though I could not remember any of my experiences. In those early days, I soon enrolled in a six-week course in meditation and I quickly learned just how ungrounded I was the moment I closed my eyes in order to meditate. The tutor explained how I needed to learn strategies to remain grounded, but still 'go out there.' In that way, I would be able to recall everything that was given to me when I meditated.

Over the following years, I worked hard at trying to remain grounded during meditation, and I began to realize that what the tutor had told me was true. By the time I started the training to become a Crystal Healing practitioner, I had mastered it. This was extremely helpful because, as I explained in Chapter Four, the College always emphasized grounding and protection.

During my training in Crystal Healing, I learned the importance of not only being grounded during meditations, but also in everyday life and, especially, when giving healing to others. I was shown different ways of ensuring I was grounded, and these included learning about earthing crystals. The College taught me that some of us are just naturally more grounded than others. I am certain the reader knows at least one person who everyone thinks of as 'spacey.' Some people are well-grounded in day-to-day life, but become ungrounded as soon as they move into their spiritual pursuits. I believe I definitely fell into this category.

In my opinion, we must not be too critical of ourselves or others when becoming ungrounded, but we should endeavor to promote our link with the Earth Mother. Try to remember that we are spiritual beings having a physical experience; therefore, being 'out there' is far more satisfying and tempting than being earthed. It is quite a natural function for us to visit the subtle levels of existence. We just need to remind ourselves that as painful as the physical level may be, at times, we chose to come here to learn.

Appendix Seven

Elevating Crystals

All minerals that are either white or clear of color possess elevating properties. The specimens used should not be large and they can be in their rough state or carved and polished into skulls, spheres, obelisks, etc. The following is a list of some elevating examples, but it is not exhaustive:

Clear Quartz
Selenite/Gypsum
Diamond {when in its polished form}
Herkimer Diamond
Natrolite {when clear or white}
Apophyllite {when clear or white}
Strontianite {when clear or white}
Amblygonite {when clear or white}
Barite {when clear or white}
Brucite {when clear or white}
Kyanite {when clear or white}
Calcite {when clear or white}
Danburite {when clear or white}
Angelsite {when clear or white}
Dolomite {when clear or white}
Topaz {when clear or white}
Colemanite {when clear or white}
Pectolite {when clear or white}
Cerussite {when clear or white}

Hemimorphite {when clear or white}
Austinite {when clear}
Muscovite {when clear or white}
Halite {when clear or white}
Borax {when clear or white}
Opal {when clear or white}
Howlite
Milky/Snowy Quartz
White Chalcedony

These other minerals and substances have also been found to possess elevating properties:

Celestite {usually pale blue, but can also be found in clear or white}
Amethyst
Sugilite
Kunzite {when purple}
Lepidolite {when lilac}
Dumortierite {when violet}
Apatite {when violet, clear, or white}
White Coral
Mother-of-Pearl
An item of Pure Gold
An item of Pure Silver

An elevating crystal or item should be placed 6-7 inches above the top of the head so that it rests beyond, and not within, a person's Crown Chakra. It is to be positioned immediately after the placing of an earthing crystal and before any other crystals are arranged and/or used elsewhere. It is the penultimate crystal or item to be removed at the end of a session.

N. B. Do not forget to cleanse elevating crystals and gold/silver items before and after use.

Other Elevating Strategies:

Pursuing such disciplines as Meditation, Yoga and Tai Chi will aid in the elevation of a person's subtle anatomy. Short-term fasting will temporarily remove the earthing properties of food from the body and, therefore, will promote better access to the spiritual realms of existence. Also, spending some time in service to others on a voluntary basis will strengthen the link between the physical ego and the Higher Self.

Appendix Eight

Using Tumblestones as Divination Tools

- On a sheet of plain paper draw a large circle and divide it into sections of between 2 and 8. {More than the latter number might create sections that are too narrow.}
- Write words in each section that signify what that area is expressing. Suggestions: "Yes—No—Not At This Time—Patience Is Needed—Excellent Outcome—Not Advisable."
- Place the paper on a table.
- Choose between 1 and 4 cleansed tumblestones of the same mineral.
- Bring the tumblestones to the table and sit down facing the paper.
- While holding the tumblestones in your receptive hand, close your eyes and take a few minutes to connect with them.
- Silently or aloud request their help in answering whatever you might ask.
- Transfer the tumblestones into your projective hand and ask your first question.
- Now gently throw the tumblestones onto the paper.
- Open your eyes and see into which sections they have landed. {If using only one tumblestone, the answer will be quite clear.}
- If using more than one, accept the answer from the section that has the most tumblestones.
- If the tumblestones indicate two, three, or even four answers, see if at least two agree and accept those. E.g. "Yes" together with "Excellent Outcome," or "No" together with "Patience Is Needed."

- Ignore any tumblestones that land outside the circle, they do not count. Only look at those within the circle. Should they all land outside, throw again.
- Ask further questions by repeating the same moves as explained above.
- When finished, thank and cleanse the tumblestones.

Appendix Nine

How to Build and Disassemble
an Etheric Structure

When building an etheric pyramid or dome, you should hold the belief that form follows thought and intention. This will strengthen your ability to create a structure at the Etheric Level. Either building should be constructed over the location of whatever metaphysical pursuit is taking place, e.g. over a chair, a massage couch, an area of a room. Also, be aware that the structure should not be too little or too large. Small etheric buildings will feel claustrophobic and lofty ones may interfere with the ability to remain earthed for both you and the client. Most importantly, if the pyramid or dome is to be positioned over anyone other than you, do not begin to build it until s/he is sitting or lying down within the assigned area.

The Pyramid:

In order to construct an etheric pyramid it is best to use 4 Baby Herkimer Diamonds or 4 AAA+ grade quality Clear Quartz tumblestones. As previously explained, Herkimer Diamonds are not diamonds. They are Clear Quartz crystals of pristine clarity that display many facets. If neither Baby Herkimers nor high grade Clear Quartz tumblestones are available, then 4 small, high grade crystal clusters or tumblestones of the same mineral and which are available to you can be substituted.

- Imagine the base perimeters of this designated space as being in the shape of a square and place a crystal/cluster/tumblestone in each of the four corners of this square. You can start with any corner, it is your choice. Use a clockwise motion to place them. These four crystals are the cornerstones for the etheric pyramid that you are about to construct.

- Stand inside the chosen area, lift your hands high above your head and close your eyes. Next, ask to be given an etheric crystal that will form the capstone of your pyramid. If you are inwardly visual, you will 'see' it. If you are not, you may be able to 'feel' it with your hands, e.g. a sense of heat or cold, a prickly sensation, a tingling in the palms. Do not have any pre-conceived ideas of what your etheric crystal will be, just trust and you will be pleasantly surprised.

- Open your eyes and hold your arms outstretched on either side of you. Now, position the palms of your hands in the direction of two cornerstones that are diagonal to each other, one hand to each stone. With intention, imagine your palms are connecting with these two cornerstones. You may get some type of sensation in your palms or fingertips. Slowly, bring your hands up to your etheric crystal, and then bring them back down to the point of their connection with the two cornerstones. Repeat this motion twice more and know that you are beginning to construct the walls of your pyramid.

- Again with intention, and in the same manner as above, connect the palms of your hands with the other two cornerstones that are diagonal to each other. Repeat the triple action as above, knowing you are completing the construction of your pyramid. If you place your open hands gently on the pyramid's walls, you can 'feel' them.

- Be aware that reverse etheric pyramids, point to point and base to base, have also formed above and below your pyramid, and that these go on ad infinitum. Therefore, ask that these further etheric structures in no way adversely affect people, animals and plants that are above or below where you are, e.g. bedrooms, cellars, apartments or offices above and below. This request can be extended to life forms within the planet or out in space.

- The walls of etheric structures are vibrating at a higher frequency than that of physical matter. Therefore, if people repeatedly pass through those walls, it is possible for them to sustain some damage to their subtle anatomy, their auric field. That is why you should build the pyramid around another person rather than constructing it before s/he goes inside it. With this in mind, it is advisable to place an etheric doorway in one of the walls of the pyramid. Then, if the other person needs to leave the structure for any reason before it is disassembled, you can direct her/him through the doorway. Build this etheric exit in whatever way feels right to you, e.g. with intention trace the shape of the doorway with your dominant/projective hand, or even visualize a door. An etheric doorway will not allow negativity to enter the pyramid; its vibrational frequency is just a little less intense than that of the walls.

- If you have been attuned to Reiki Level II or above, you can go round and trace, then blow, the Sei-He-Ki onto the outside of each of the four pyramidal walls. The Sei-He-Ki provides powerful protection.
- Finally, ask that what happens within the pyramid is right and appropriate for those who spend time within its dimensions.

You can now enter the pyramid through any of the four etheric walls and remain inside or pass in and out of it, depending on the metaphysical work that is taking place. As the builder/creator of the pyramid, your energy vibration is 'in tune' with that of the structure and you should not experience any ill effects from repeatedly passing through the walls. However, if you are concerned that your subtle bodies might be damaged by moving in and out of the pyramid, then either utilize the etheric doorway or create another opening in one of the other three walls before entering or exiting the pyramid.

It should not be necessary to reinforce the structure of the pyramid while it is in existence. However, if there is a time when you feel this action is needed, it can be done quickly by connecting the four cornerstones to the etheric crystal once again. The previous hand movements are not needed. You can just use the power of your mind and visualization.

N. B. It is very important not to leave etheric structures in place once their protective and stabilizing properties are no longer required. When they remain intact, they become stronger and more permanent. This means the longer they exist the more difficult it becomes to fully remove them. In addition, the vibrational frequency of their walls intensifies and will cause greater tears and holes within the auric fields of those who pass through them. Eventually, this adverse effect could also impact on the person who constructed them because the walls' energy vibration will no longer be in harmony with their builder. The following instructions will remove the etheric pyramid and should be conducted as soon as the metaphysical pursuit is ended.

- While standing inside the pyramid, hold your hands above your head in order to connect, once more, with your etheric crystal. Close your eyes and 'see' or 'feel' yourself holding this celestial capstone. Give the crystal your thanks and send it back to its etheric home with a little pushing motion.
- Open your eyes and move outside the pyramid. Pick up the four cornerstones in the reverse order from which you placed them and give each one your thanks. This action and the removal of the etheric crystal will automatically disassemble the pyramid. The crystals/clusters/tumblestones will also need cleansing as soon as you have removed the pyramid.
- With a large feather, or your hands, or any other way that feels appropriate, sweep into a bundle any excess energy/residue bits and pieces of the pyramid that you sense are remaining. Do not fling this bundle just anywhere, either by hand actions or visualization. Instead, send it with love and a gentle hand motion either up to the Divine or down to the Earth Mother. In this way, the remaining energy will be transmuted to its highest form or stabilized by grounding rather than having been thrown somewhere to just hang around and degrade into negative energy.
- Thank the Divine, the archangels and angels; also remember to give your thanks to the mineral kingdom.

The Dome:

When constructing a dome, you can use Baby Herkimer Diamonds, Clear Quartz tumbles, or any good quality, small mineral clusters or tumblestones. The usual number of foundation stones for a dome is 8, but you can use 10 or even 12 if you prefer.

- Position the foundation stones, one by one, in a circle around the designated space. You can begin in whatever part of the circle you like and should be using a clockwise motion to place them.

- Stand inside the encircled area and, with eyes closed, lift your hands high above your head. Now, ask to be given an etheric crystal which will form the top focal point on the curve of your dome. If you are inwardly visual, you will 'see' it. If you are not, you may be able to 'feel' it with your hands; the same examples of 'feeling' the crystal apply as given in the construction of an etheric pyramid. Remember, do not have any pre-conceived ideas of what your etheric crystal will be, just trust that you are being given the right one.

- Open your eyes and bring your arms down to an outstretched position on either side of you. Place your palms in the directions of two foundation stones that are diagonal to each other. With intention, imagine your palms are connecting with these two stones. You may get some type of sensation in your palms or fingertips. Slowly, bring your hands up to your etheric crystal and then bring them back down to the point of their connection with the two foundation stones. Repeat this connecting motion twice more and know that you have begun to construct the dome.

- Then, continuing around the circle, repeat this triple connecting motion for the remainder of the stones, two at a time. When you have completed the dome, you can gently 'feel' the circular wall of your etheric building. Also be aware that, unlike an etheric pyramid, reverse domes will not have manifested ad infinitum.

- Re-read the information given in Bullet Point #6 for building an etheric pyramid. That information applies to any type of etheric construction. Build a doorway somewhere in the dome's curved wall, following the instructions given previously.

- If you have been attuned to Reiki Level II or above, you can trace, and then blow, the Sei-He-Ki onto the outside of the dome's wall. You can move around and repeat this action more than once, if this feels right to you. The Sei-He-Ki always brings powerful protection.

- Finally, ask that what happens within the dome is right and appropriate for those who spend time within its extent.

You can now enter the dome through its wall and remain inside or pass in and out of it, depending on the metaphysical work that is taking place. As the builder/creator of the dome, your energy vibration is comparable with that of the structure and you should not experience any ill effects from repeatedly passing through the walls. However, if you are concerned that your subtle bodies might be damaged, you can either move through the etheric doorway or create another opening in another section of the dome before entering or exiting it.

As noted previously, it should not be necessary to reinforce the structure of the dome while it is in existence. However, if there is a time when you feel this action is needed, this can be done quickly by reconnecting the foundation stones to the etheric crystal. Once again, the previous hand movements are not needed. You can just use the power of your mind and visualization.

Remember, it is very important not to leave etheric structures in place once their properties are no longer needed. Therefore, follow the disassembling instructions that were given for a pyramid in order to quickly remove all trace of the etheric dome. After releasing your etheric crystal, you will pick up the 8, 10, or 12 foundation minerals in the reverse order from which you placed them. Remember to give them your thanks and to cleanse them immediately. Do not forget to sweep away any excess energy and send it in the direction of the Divine or the Earth Mother. Lastly, show gratitude to the higher realms and the mineral kingdom.

Bibliography

Webb-De Sisto, Marion. *Crystal Skulls*, Xlibris Corporation, 2002.
Webb-De Sisto, Marion. *Soul Wisdom, Volume One*, Xlibris Corporation, 2000.
Webb-De Sisto, Marion. *Soul Wisdom, Volume Two*, Xlibris Corporation, 2003.

Relevant Contact Details of the Featured People and Training Facilities in this Book

People:

Sue Bouvier
Registered Crystal Healing Practitioner—Druid Priestess—Tarot Card Reader—Crystal/Crystal Skull Worker & Collector.
Location: United Kingdom.
Email: *soubou1@aol.com*

Linda Cody
B.A in Psychology—M.A. in Divinity—Paranormal Investigator—Crystal/ Crystal Skull Worker & Collector.
Location: High Point, North Carolina, U.S.A.
Email: Private.

Jeanne Simpson Dunn
Spiritual Woman—Psychic Reader/Empath—Crystal/Crystal Skull Worker & Collector—Writer & Artist.
Location: U.S.A.
Email: *jeanze@comcast.net*
MySpace: *http://www.myspace.com/jeanze*
Website *{under construction}*: *http://www.jeanze.com*

Helena Albrecht-Esperandieu.
Angelic Reiki Master—Crystal/Crystal Skull Worker & Collector—Artist.
Location: France/South Africa.
Email: *hesperandieu@yahoo.com*
Website: *http://perso.wanadoo.fr/hesperandieu/*

Mark Loman
Shaman—Elestial Reiki Master—Crystal/Crystal Skull Worker &
Collector—Tarot Card Reader—Goldsmith.
Location: United Kingdom.
Email: *mark@yumyumi.freeserve.co.uk*

Douglas Ratcliff.
Crystal/Crystal Skull Worker & Collector.
Location: U.S.A.
Email: *maplebob23@yahoo.com*

Elaine Simmons
M.Ed. in Counseling—Certified Clinical Hypnotherapist—Reiki
Practitioner—Tarot Card & Astrology Reader—Crystal/Crystal Skull
Worker & Collector.
Location: U.S.A.
Email: Private.

Lisa Trevethan.
Alchemy's Muse Vibrational Essences & Alchemy.
Location: U.S.A.
Email: *alchemuse@digitalsidhe.com*
Website: *http://www.digitalsidhe.com/amwelcome.htm*

Deb Chenneour Williams.
Certified in Hypnotherapy, Past-Life Regression & Transpersonal
Psychology—Spiritual Life Coach—Crystal/Crystal Skull
Worker & Collector.
Location: Mendota, IL. U.S.A.
Email: *wyllow69@yahoo.com*
MySpace: *http://profile.myspace.com/index.cfm?fuseaction=user.viewprofile&fr
iendid=122537276*

Twitter: *https://twitter.com/home*
FaceBook: *http://www.facebook.com/profile.php?id=1285476430*

Andrea Wright.
Reiki Practitioner—Tarot Card Reader—Distant Healer—Crystal/Crystal Skull Worker & Collector.
Location: United Kingdom
Email: *winterbabes24@yahoo.co.uk*

Training Facilities:

The International College of Crystal Healing.
Location: United Kingdom.
ACHO Affiliation Website: *http://www.crystal-healing.org/ICCH.htm*

The Warrior in the Heart Shamanism.
Location: c/o Isle of Avalon Foundation
2-4 High Street
Glastonbury
Somerset, BA6 9DU
United Kingdom.
Email: *warriorintheheart@tiscali.co.uk*
Website: *http://www.shamanicwarrior.com*

Two Fantasy Novels by
Marion Webb-De Sisto

Samael's Fall: The Angelic Chronicles—Xlibris Corporation 2005.
ISBN—Softcover: 1-4134-9114-6; Hardcover: 1-4134-9115-4

> He is handsome, charismatic and a radiant celestial being,
> but he is rapidly becoming a dark soul.

This book is a stirring account of how and why the first and most radiant archangel fell from grace and became the Devil. It is a story of angels and demons, love and hate, goodness and evil. Religion has taught us that the archangels and angels are extremely wise and have faultless purity. However, this is not the author's controversial portrayal of them. These heavenly beings possess a child-like quality; they make mistakes and use poor judgment. This first novel of *The Angelic Chronicles* trilogy is a blending of fantasy with esoteric teachings. It has been placed in the top 100 of Amazon's Category Sales Ranks for books about the Occult.

Abbadon: Book Two of The Angelic Chronicles—Xlibris Corporation 2007.
ISBN—Softcover: 978-1-4257-9865-9; Hardcover: 978-1-4257-9918-2

> Become reacquainted with the first and seventh archangelic brothers,
> Samael and Seriel, in their further celestial exploits.

Both siblings have been exiled to Abbadon, a dark, hellish place where essence-drinking demons and energy-sapping plant life abound. There is even a fierce, golden dragon to breathe fire into the story. The brothers' rivalry continues to exist between them as they adjust to being separated from their beloved Malkura. Each handles this misfortune in his own way. Seriel is resigned to never having won her affection while Samael plots to regain what he has lost. He also discovers a crystal with which he can extract souls. *Book Two* has something for everyone; there is plenty of adventure, romance and some dastardly deeds by Samael, a.k.a. the Devil.

LaVergne, TN USA
28 September 2009
159246LV00010B/179/P